Divining
Archaeology

by

Walter Elliot

DEDICATION

To all archaeologists, professional and amateur, who have doubted my veracity and sanity. Without their studied indifference, the following would never have appeared in book form.

ISBN No. 978-0-9561075-9-6

Published by Bordersprint Ltd., Selkirk TD7 4DG

CONTENTS

Acknowledgements

Preface

ACKNOWLEDGEMENTS

This book is written by Kay's Rules, i.e., '*What I can do, I will do; when I need help, I will ask for it*'. Amongst those who volunteered assistance/made suggestions were Brian Appleby, John and Margaret Collin, Helen Darling, Rob Elliot, Donald Gordon, Fraser Hunter, Alistair Moffat, Debbie Playfair and Richard Strathie.

Thanks to the metal detectorists who have added so much to the history and archaeology of the Borders – Michael Brown, George Burns, Billy Butler, Roger Elliot, Jock Graham, Kenny Holisz, Ian McGeorge, Jim Middleton, Bill Slight, Scott Sibbald, Paul and Brenda Smith et alii.

I am grateful to **The Southern Reporter** for the use of the cover photograph which was taken nearly twenty years ago by Gordon Lockie, and to the Peeblesshire Archaeological Society for use of their map of the possible temporary camp at Darnhall.

Most thanks are due to James and Cath Rutherford for undertaking the tidying-up, layout and publication of the book.

PREFACE

In '*Selkirkshire and The Borders, Book One*', I used the term 'divining rods' as one of my source materials but never got round to giving a detailed description of how they worked as an archaeological search device for me.

In this book, I will be re-visiting some of the sites with some visual aids to re-evaluate my previous conclusions and in some cases will quote my arguments from Selkirkshire to make a rounded picture.

Although I had always been interested in the history of the countryside around me, in the mid-1950s I started to take an active interest in finding out more about it. By field-walking, I could get in touch with the past, literally. This produced relics from all ages, but was then regarded by some as 'scavenging' or 'magpie collecting'. Twenty years later it became customary to field-walk a site before starting an excavation.

In the 1980s, the use of a metal detector was branded by the short-sighted as 'destroying the nation's heritage', 'vandals', 'treasure hunters' etc. and that metal detectorists should be jailed, if not executed. The resultant vitriolic wars between some professional archaeologists and detectorists resulted in many important finds and sites remaining unreported. Regrettably, this debate has been firmly implanted in the minds of some of the protagonists.

However by 2010, about ninety-five per cent of the metal finds in Scotland are made by detectorists. These are reported, noted and written up; then returned to the finder or claimed as a national treasure with the finder receiving the monetary equivalent. This way everybody wins.

By publishing sites found by divining, I write not for riches, glory or honours but only to pass on my finds and ideas for others to use. By pinpointing the areas where air photographers and geophysicists can look for patterns in the ground and fieldwalkers and metal detectorists may find positive proofs that my ideas are not as mad as they might seem. What I have written may not be accepted at present but there is nothing unbelievable herein.

Walter Elliot

CHAPTER ONE

Introduction to Divining

'Dowse' – to use a divining rod – *n* Dowser, a water diviner

'Divining rod' – a rod usually of hazel, used by those professing to discover water or metal under ground.

Chambers Twentieth Century Dictionary. 1943

To write about divining was always going to be difficult. Getting normal people to believe that a somewhat staid individual could get two pieces of L-shaped fencing wire to indicate what is under the ground, stretches belief to near breaking point – and past it in many cases. To suggest that the same pieces of wire could pick out people by name from a crowd of strangers, would normally require the attendance of two muscular nurses and a strait-jacket; but yet they do.

I have been using this technique to investigate the little-known or unknown archaeological remains in the Borders for a long, long time. In that time I have met a few believers, have suffered the slingshots and arrows of outraged professional and amateur archaeologists and had questions raised about my sanity by others, although a few were prepared to give me the benefit of the doubt. In the final two years of the excavations at Trimontium, Dr Simon Clarke who was then in charge of the excavations, gave me the best accolade I have ever received from a professional archaeologist 'Walter, you are as mad as a hatter but you are always worth listening to'.

This was after I had convinced him that rabbits could play their part in archaeological research. On the edge of the railway cutting at Newstead, the Bradford students had discovered traces of five Roman pits. However there were two spots where three rabbit holes appeared close together. Knowing that rabbits would rather burrow in loose soil than hard, I was allowed to dig the top layers away to reveal a further two Roman pits awaiting discovery.

Moles are good too. When a ditch is dug and filled in, it retains moisture better than the surrounding tightly-packed earth and this attracts worms. Moles like worms and trace them along the lines of the former ditch, making mole-hills as they go. So a line of molehills may indicate a former ditch, be it a field drain or a Roman fort outer defence. I have to thank a family of moles for bringing to my attention a series of squarish blocks of molehills which indicated that the 'grubenhausen' of a 5th/7th century Anglian settlement lay under the surface at a site near Ettrickbridgend.

There will be an extended use of the first person singular in what follows below because this is a personal journey through the ages and nobody else would knowingly wish to be associated with the views stated. I don't apologise for this as I am sure the use of divining rods can be used to extend the scope of archaeology in the Borders and elsewhere.

In fact, dowsing/divining for water or metal had been practiced in many countries over many centuries.

The Bible, Numbers, chapter 21, verses 7-11 reads:

And the Lord spake unto Moses saying
Take the rod and gather thou the assembly together, thou and Aaron thy brother
and speak ye unto the rock before their eyes; and thou shall bring forth to them
water out of the rock; so thou shalt give the congregation and their beasts drink.
And Moses took the rod from before the Lord as He commanded him.
And Moses and Aaron gathered the congregation together before the rock, and he
said unto them 'Hear now, ye rebels; must we fetch you water out of this rock?'
And Moses lifted his hand and with his rod he smote the rock twice and water
came out abundantly and the congregation drank, and their beasts also.

This is taken to be a miracle but it is a graphic description of a diviner finding water where there were no visible signs to convinced a doubting population. It must be remembered that The Old Testament is basically a compiled history of the Jewish people and a man who could find water during a forty-year journey through the desert, was worthy of note.

To the public mind, divining or dowsing is usually associated with the search for water. In medieval Britain and the Continent, there are instances of castle wells being dug through many metres of solid rock to get to the pure water that the diviners said was there. This shows a great faith in the certainty of the diviners.

In Scotland, the most obvious examples are the Fore Well of Edinburgh Castle, the Draw or Holy Well of Inchcolm Abbey and wells of the medieval abbey of St Andrews which sits out on a rocky headland.

Despite the fact that dowsing rods were known to produce the required results, the Church was very wary about the means. With no reasonable explanation, dowsing was looked on as a form of witchcraft and had to be discouraged. There are many written examples of rods being used by diviners and the results tested by examiners but although the results were almost totally positive, the Church kept its reservations. Any well found by divining was bound to be a miracle and therefore the wells were Holy Wells.

In medieval Europe, divining was a practical method for miners to locate metal ores without the trouble of digging trial trenches all over the countryside. In 1556, Georgius Agricola published a book on mining and the methods of smelting ore. In it, is a description of dowsing for ore and a detailed woodcut showing two men using Y-shaped divining rods. This book *De Re Metallica* was so highly prized that copies were chained to the pulpit in German churches and read to the illiterate miners by the parish priests. Yet Agricola, aware of the bigotry of that age, advised that *'a miner, since he ought to be a good and serious man, should not make use of the enchanted twig'*. This was only window-dressing and the German and Balkan miners quietly ignored the advice.

In 1692, there is a well-documented case of a French peasant called Aymer who tracked the murderers of a rich wine merchant and his wife from Lyons to Toulon by divining. This was taken up by the investigative press of the day and Aymer was given many tests which he passed with flying colours. One of the 'Red Top' papers of the time asked him to walk through certain street to see if he could finds any houses where the ladies 'had soiled their honour'. When he naively obliged, the gutter press had a field day and a community spirit was lost forever.

During the Vietnam War, the American Army used dowsing to locate Viet-cong underground tunnels, stores and booby-traps. However in 1968, after six dowsers gave a hundred per cent success demonstration before the Army Command, the skills were dismissed because nobody could explain scientifically why it worked.

Dowsing or divining rods can be used for many purposes in medicine, diagnosing allergies, soil testing, finding objects or people but it is regarded with great suspicion by scientists and others who are more interested in why it works, rather than whether it works. This attitude is very prevalent in the Archaeological Establishment.

My own purpose in writing this book is to let others know that there are still many archaeological sites in the Borders and a lot more information about its past waiting to be gleaned by whatever means. Archaeology tends to concentrate on modern methods of discovery, air photography, geophysics, carbon dating etc. while discarding the natural methods of the past.

CHAPTER TWO

Early Days

Although born in Selkirk, my first fourteen years were spent in Ettrick at the Oakwood and Fauldshope farms; then two years at Prieston near Midlem and finally at Lindean on the Sunderland Hall Estate. The reason for moving was that my father was a fencing contractor and we were dependent on a vacant farm cottage for housing. If the house was needed for a farm worker, we moved on. The family was still at Lindean when I left Selkirk High School and I did some time as a fencer before going to serve National Service, first at the K.O.S.B. depot at Berwick and then with the 1st Battalion in Northern Ireland. I got de-mobbed on 3rd November 1954, checked in my kit at the 4th Battalion HQ in Galashiels as a further three and a half years with the Territorials was part of the contract, and started work as a fencing contractor on 5th November.

In those days, field and hill fences were usually five plain wires with a barb on top. To get a good strain on the wires, a six ratchet machine was used, so the end posts had to be placed about 1.4m into the ground and packed around with stones to take the strain. Digging a 30cm square posthole to that depth meant two to three hours hard work for there were no post drivers available then. Digging the hole was hard but quite do-able unless you happened to hit and break a tile drain which was inconveniently lurking about 60cm below the ground surface. Break that and the whole drainage system of the field spilled out into your posthole. This water had to be baled out, the broken tile replaced, the soil filled in again and a new posthole started a couple of metres away. When this happened it was a wasted day that caused much annoyance and some rude words.

A solution presented itself in 1966. While visiting my field-walking friends, Jack and Caroline Cruickshank, I saw their gardener, Mr Cornwall, using two L-shaped pieces of wire to find where the water-pipes were around the house. I had seen these in use on farms before but had never tried them myself. On trying them, I discovered that they worked for me, wobbly at first but getting better through practice. With them I could find the locations of field drains in order to avoid them. Great.

A further development waited. If a farmer wanted a fence on the site where there had previously been one even although there were no surface signs, I could ask the divining rods where the nearest posthole was. Asking two pieces of fencing wire where a previous post had been sounds a bit weird but when they pointed in one direction and crossed at one place, I could confidently take the sod off and jack out the rotten stump of the previous post. This allowed me to slide in the new post and saved two hours digging. Even better.

In time I discovered that I could find the locations of ancient postholes and by marking out their individual locations, could get the pattern of the posts of a Bronze Age roundhouse or an Anglian hall. By extending their scope, I could locate temporary Roman camps, find their rubbish pits and tell which way their tents were facing through the location of their tent-poles.

I realised that post stumps had their own story to tell. As a practical fencing contractor, I knew that any stumps removed from the fence line could not be older than 160 years when wire fencing came to the Borders.

In clay or peaty soil, the end/corner posts of a fence were dug 1.4m into the ground. Although they rot at ground level, the stump of the post is often as sound as the day it went in ground; and this extends into the ancient past. When the Roman fort at Oakwood was excavated in 1952, the posts of the east gate were found to be in good condition. If these had been found in a modern dig, they would have been subject to dendrochronology (the study of tree ring growths), radio carbon dating and pollen analysis. This would have told us when the tree was cut, the time of year it was placed in the ground and what plants were growing in the vicinity.

So when I find where posts once stood, I know that a great deal of knowledge lies under my feet.

With more practice, I discovered that I could differentiate between the various disturbances under the ground. This was handy while erecting garden fences. In a house, there are water and electric pipes coming in and sewage going out; to hit one of these with a pinch-bar caused a great deal of inconvenience. So I discovered that I could find one, say water, then look for the electric supply and then the sewage drain. By this method the rods would first find and then ignore the water pipe and only crossed where the electric supply entered the house; and so on to the sewer pipe while ignored the previous two lines. Weird but true. This sounds total fantasy but it worked every time, so much so that eventually I could tell what material was in the trenches – tile, lead, copper, iron, plastic etc. This I usually kept quiet about, as my reputation for eccentricity was growing. But this is not unusual as I know several people who can do the same.

I never questioned the theory of how divining rods worked, they just did. If I had to make a reasonable explanation, I would suggest that they indicate soil disturbance through water collection. When ground is dug, even although the soil is replaced immediately, it is not so firmly packed as the surrounding undisturbed earth and rainwater tends to filter in and collect there. This shows up in air photographs during a dry year and is the basis of geophysics where a machine records the strength of the reflected electrical current as it bounces back through the ground.

To explain why humans may react in the same way, some scientists have formed a theory known as the 'ideomotor effect' where the subconscious mind can influence human sensitivity without the person being consciously aware of it; and this is reflected by the rods crossing. I still prefer my own explanation.

One thing I did notice was that whatever influence caused the rods to cross, it did not come up through the feet and body but only happened when the hands were above the object/target. By standing near a drain or posthole and projecting the hands forward, it is possible to get its exact position. When all the postholes have been marked, the size and shape of a long-vanished wooden building can be determined even although there are no signs of it on the ground surface.

Many farms of my youth had a man who could divine for drains, while the Water Board workers and most plumbers used the same technique to locate water pipes. They were practical labour-saving devices which cut down on unproductive searching time.

Most diviners use the two pieces of L-shaped wires that cross over the target. Others use a single straight rod of hazel, sometimes known as a 'wand' and doubtless the forerunner of the magic wand used by Harry Potter and storybook enchanters. The single rod either dips or vibrates while passing over the drain or water pipe. This does not work for me at all.

My maternal grandfather used a Y-shaped hazel branch with most spectacular results. His party piece was to stuff a cushion down the front of his waist-coat, then hold the two legs of the branch very loosely in his hands and walk over a drain. The branch came up to hit his chest so strongly that it would have given him a severe bruising; hence the cushion. We used to try to hold the branch but couldn't unless one leg of the branch left his hand; then it reverted to being a small hazel twig.

I would never have regarded divining rods as anything other than useful aids to avoiding field drains and detecting the sites of previously dug postholes if it had not been for excavations at the Roman fort of Trimontium near Newstead.

I had field-walked the site since 1955, originally with Bruce and Walter Mason, later with Jack and Caroline Cruickshank and over the years had acquired a large number of Roman artefacts, some of which did not fit in with what was already known. These I wrote up and published as short notes in Proceedings of the Society of Antiquaries of Scotland as I considered that new knowledge is like old muck – no use unless it is spread around.

In the mid-1980s, Mark Gillings, a student in the Department of Archaeological Studies of Bradford University was studying for a PhD on Roman pottery made in Scotland. I had been finding sherds of misshapen pottery with the stamps EMI and INVOM:ANDVS in the fields of Newstead, and had come to the logical conclusion that they were potters working near the fort of Trimontium. When Mark called to see the broken pots (wasters), they were exactly what he was looking for and he told his tutor, Dr Rick Jones about all the other objects we had found on the site.

One thing led to another and soon we were planning a series of excavations on the Roman fort and its relationship with the local native settlements. The Bradford Department of Archaeological Sciences was keen to try out their relatively recent geophysics equipment and this was an ideal place. The basics of geophysics is that an electrical impulse is shot into the ground and the strength of the returning signal recorded. A similar machine, the magnetometer, records the magnetic impulses in the ground. Variations in ground readings produce patterns to tell whether there is a ditch or a hard surface underneath. The first trial dig was in September 1987 and was successful enough to warrant further exploration.

With encouragement from all sides, a larger area was opened next year. I was digging in company with Kenny Holisz, a local electrician, and divining rods were mentioned. He said that he used them in some parts of his work. I think it was on his suggestion that we decided to try them out on the site; and they worked beautifully. Soon I was finding ditches and building foundations but could not convince the professional archaeologists who, after all, were scientists.

They were quite prepared to accept the rods for water and drain divining, but when I used the same methods using the rods as archaeological search machines, this was totally unbelievable; yet there was little difference between finding a 0.3m wide drain 0.8m deep and a Roman Fort outer ditch which was 7 metres wide and 3 to 4 metres deep. I have been, and still get "leg-pulled" by archaeologists over my use of divining rods – but they work for me, almost all the time. And the finds are in no way contaminated by the methods used in their discovery.

During the ten-year excavations at Trimontium, I was called in several times to find pits and ditches which James Curle had already excavated and mapped but which did not show up on the geophysics plotting. Acceptance of divining rods was conceded in 1993 when an area of the south annexe of the fort was being laid out for excavation. This was known to include pit XVII excavated by Curle in November 1905. It was six feet six inches in diameter at the surface and thirty-one feet nine inches deep. Unfortunately it did not show up on the geophysics plot even although its exact location was noted on Curle's plan of the site. Two minutes with divining rods had it placed just where Curle said it was. Then Rick Jones had to admit that he *'knew that dowsing could work in some ways and up to a point for some people'* – not the greatest of plaudits but welcome just the same. But he still did not trust the evidence of 'twitching twigs'.

(Subversively, I got the students to try out the rods and they worked for three out of four. I did warn them not to quote the results on any exam papers.)

Later on in the excavations, the geophysics plots of the west annexe of the fort, showed that the Roman baths at Trimontium which Curle had dug and photographed, seemed to have disappeared between 1910 and 1990,* but the explanation that the large stones in the truncated walls *'may have been ploughed out'* did not convince me. They are still there. Conclusion - The scientific worlds are often reluctant to accept anything which does not conform to their own accepted ideas of the truth.

* I have to acknowledge that the geophysics of the late 1980s and early 1990s have been superseded by ground-penetrating radar of the 2010s.

I know that divining rods are not infallible. Some years ago, I found a perfect Roman fortlet on Dere Street near Mount Hooly and a watch tower on the other side of the road. I was so sure of it that I got another diviner to check my findings, with the same results. When I used a JCB to put a trench through the ditches, I expected the black soil with bits of pottery and bones that were common in the Trimontium trenches. Instead I was presented with some shallow depressions in the face of the cutting, but nothing convincing. So I paid £150 and put it down to experience. It was only in 2011/12, when I was plotting out the fortlets along Dere Street that I found a space where there should have been a fortlet. So I went back and found it was still there – I had misread the ground.

As well as my own mistakes, some strange things happen when the divining rods seem to take on a mind of their own. Take two instances. About ten years ago, I was plodding along a very minor unknown Roman road south of Bowden. Roads are easy to trace as, if you wander off the line, the rods will turn to left or right to guide you back on track again. In this instance, I was going past a ploughed field when the rods veered abruptly to the right and, as is my wont, I followed their line for some thirty metres before they crossed. When I looked down, there was a small piece of red-glazed Samian pottery about the size of my thumb nail. This is now in the National Museum.

Certainly it would be easy for me to fake evidence by finding a piece at Trimontium and saying that I had found it near Bowden. I don't do things like that owing to an inherent honesty and the fact that it would distort the history of the Borders.

In 2010, a hoard of Roman silver coins were found about half a kilometre from where the divining rods pointed out the small piece of pottery, so there has been some Roman activity in the native settlements around Trimontium.

Four years ago, I was asked to locate a water track on a farm between Reston and Preston. I don't usually do anything like that because it could become very time-consuming and I am approaching the stage where time is a precious and decreasing commodity, but in this case said that I would.

I was plodding up the hill quite happily on the old water supply track when the rods turned abruptly. Thinking it might be a feeder track I followed it but could find no trace of a pipe or drain. Instead the rods crossed over a very small stone bead on top of a turf turned over by a tractor wheel. I knew exactly what it was as I had found another forty years before on The Yair Hill, Selkirkshire. This bead was made from lithomarge, a soft rock which is a mixture of red, white and grey stone and could be dated to 1st century BC/1st century AD. It is one of twelve or so which have been found in Scotland and the north of England. Although I kept it for a few months to admire, it is now in the National Museum as a national treasure.

Why these two objects drew the attention of the divining rods, I have no idea because I was not looking for pottery or unusual beads. It has been suggested that some people have a natural affinity to the ground without being aware of it. Certainly I know at least three metal detectorists who go on to the most unpromising sites and come off with rare or unique objects. *'There are more things in heaven and earth, Horatio'* etc.

So, in venturing into the shoogly moss of archaeology with the claim that divining rods can give indications of sites and objects that even the most modern scientific machines cannot, I am aware that the dark clouds of Establishment wrath will loom over me.

What follows below is not a vague belief but a firm conviction. All I ask is that minds are kept open to the results, rather than condemning the methods. I was once told by an Inspector of Ancient Monuments that any new idea in archaeology had to be strained through fifty years of doubt before becoming accepted. Obviously an optimist!

I have adopted the outlook of Arthur Schopenhauer (1788-1860), a German philosopher known for his pessimism and his belief that the world was not a rational place: *'All truth passes through three stages. First, it is ridiculed. Second, it is violently opposed. Third, it is accepted as self-evident.'* I am midway between ridicule and violent opposition of sceptics whose belief in their own intellectual superiority is unshakeable. In time, things may change.

I have to admit that I use divining rods in conjunction with any other clues that are available in the landscape. These might be marks in the ground that I had noted during fencing operations, folklore, concentrations of field-walking finds and air photographs.

Documents, air photographs, geophysics in its various forms, carbon-dating, pollen analysis, metal detecting, divining, fieldwalking and casual finds give clues to our archaeological and historical past. But it is the spade and trowel that provides the proof although even these proofs can also be misread. Basically, we are all guessers at what might have happened. Sometimes the guesses are wildly romanticised, exaggerated or simply misread.

In the winter of 1846, a railway cutting was made through what is now known to be the south annexe of the Roman Fort at Newstead. Among a number of pits and wells found during the digging, one contained the skeleton of a man *'erect or nearly so at the bottom of a pit ten to twelve feet deep and three or four feet in diameter'*. This fired the imagination and the story went that he was faithfully guarding the Roman frontier, while local legend had his ghost parading along the limits of the fort.

Reality is likely to be more prosaic. Probably the poor squaddie was digging a pit when the sides fell in and suffocated him before he could be rescued. His comrades, rather than dig him out for re-burial or cremation, simply filled in the hole and left him to be discovered by the navvies many centuries later.

DIVINING HUMANS – THE LIVING AND THE DEAD

In the public mind, anyone with divining rods is thought to be looking for water but in fact, they can be used in other ways like tracing illness and allergies in humans or plants or searching for objects. Some of the practitioners are genuine and produce good results; some are not.

Although I can find objects, my best results are with people. One of my party pieces was brought out when students of the Department of Celtic Studies at Edinburgh University come for a day to look at the Celtic sites/placenames in the Borders.

I would meet them at Newstead to take them along the site of the Roman Fort. Along the road to the fort, I would tell them about divining rods and how it was possible to find the ditches and ramparts of the fort with them. My demonstration was usually viewed with scepticism. However, when I produced several pairs of rods and got them to try, it was discovered that about three in four were able to use them with some degree of proficiency. Some simply refused to touch the rods as if they would bite.

There was even more scepticism and a gentle movement away from me when I said I could find people with the rods. I would then get a name and the rods pointed to that person – and immediately get accused of fraud, that I had already found out the name for somebody in the party.

So I lined them up in a row, turned my back on them and asked the most vocal critic to give me a name. The rods pointed over my shoulder to the person named – fewer doubts this time. So I did it again with the same result. I never tried it more than twice because you never know what the magical number three might do. (I am kidding.)

On one of the trips, there was a lady tutor who was so violently opposed to the whole idea that she refused to believe anything she saw, nor would she touch the divining rods. Eventually she was persuaded to hold the rods to prove that the whole thing was a fraud – and they worked beautifully. At that moment, she turned from a sophisticated University lecturer to an excited thirteen-year-old girl.

Some thirty years ago, I was putting up a new fence on Philiphaugh Farm on the edge of the Cricket Field and The Orchard (now the Football Field). While doing my normal search for former postholes, the rods kept going sideways and marking out small plots of 2m by 0.80m. Knowing that I was on the site of the Battle of Philiphaugh, I thought that I could be finding the graves of those killed there.

Later air photographs show that these graves were part of a cemetery and a further trip with the divining rods showed that the graveyard was enclosed by a double palisade. Inside the palisade, postholes indicate a wooden building about 10m by 4m which is likely to have been the church.

The air photographs revealed an Anglian field system and several buildings. When a Roman gold ring with an intaglio inset, was found by a metal detectorist on the same field, it was worth a further exploration with the rods. I discovered that the ring was found on the site of a large Anglian hall. This should have been more properly described as 'four rows of potential former postholes which would suggest a large Anglian Hall'. Only excavation or a very lucky air photograph will provide the answer. However the name of 'Selekirke' splits down into two Anglian words 'sele', a hall and 'kirke' a church. The Charter of Foundation of Selkirk Abbey in 1119 AD, refers to 'the old town beside the Ettrick'.

In 2011, the Battle of Philiphaugh was being investigated by G.U.A.R.D. (Glasgow University Archaeological Research Division). To determine the extent and focal points of the battle, a number of local metal detectorists were enlisted to look for musket and pistol balls. During this survey a silver Roman seal-box lid and two pieces of Samian pottery were found. This poses more questions than it answers.

In the 1960s, we had a lot of fencing contracts in the Lammermuirs, travelling down there on Monday morning to stay in a bothy at Crichness and coming back on the Friday night. During this decade, I was driving over Greenlaw Moor, a beautiful heather-clad expanse of land that a wise owner had preserved in its natural state. On one of the journeys, I noted a number of small bumps in the heather.

It took about forty years before I got there with divining rods and found that the bumps were basically low earth mounds around three/four metres across and about half a metre high at the most. They are not stone-gather heaps as there are no/very few stones on the ground surface of this peat moor, especially on the western side of the marked area. On trying them with the rods, I found that they were burial mounds with at least one body in them; some had as many as three. This is an extensive cairnfield at **NT 714 484** that covers nearly a kilometre. The site was confirmed during a visit by Deirdre Cameron of Historic Scotland in June 2004.

On the eastern side, there are fewer actual mounds, but marker stones have been placed at the top and bottom of the divined graves – these could be the '*heid stanes* and '*fit stanes*' of the early Christian era.

The most remarkable feature of the site is a natural loch, the Hule Moss, which seems to defy the laws of nature. Measuring approximately 400 metres by 150 metres, it lies on a flat piece of ground between two slopes, north and south. However to the east and west of the loch, the ground falls away gently and it would seem easier for the water to run away than to stay where it is.

This phenomenon would almost certainly account for its Anglian/Dark Age name of the Hule or Holy Moss and might account for the heid/fit stanes of a nearby Christian? burial ground. However the unusual natural configuration and the presence of water would make it a strong candidate for a place of pagan worship before being taken over by a Christian community.

Fast forward two years and I was helping Debbie Playfair to write up a James Hutton trail through the Borders. James Hutton was the Berwickshire farmer who first put forward the proposition that the world was far older than the Biblical reckoning of time and is now acknowledged to be the Father of Geology. Debbie had been the Monuments Warden for scheduled archaeological sites in the Borders for thirteen years and in that time had acquired a lot of historical knowledge of the area.

On the way back from a photographic expedition of geological sites, we stopped to have a look at the cairnfield. Taking divining rods, we set out to prove the cairnfield. When she asked 'Can you tell whether it is the grave of a man or a woman?' I tried and found that I could. First ask one question 'Is it a male?' and if there is no response, 'Is it a female?' One of the questions was always answered with an affirmative crossing, except for the times when both questions were answered yes - obviously a man and woman. Individually, we tried ten graves without saying what we were getting and discovered that we both came up with the same answers. But nothing could be definitely proved without digging up a lot of graves and the subject remained unresolved. That is until I was asked to give a demonstration of divining at the East Berwickshire Natural History weekend – my daughter Lynne was a member of the committee.

It was a very wet weekend and I couldn't get into the field beside the Priory at Coldingham, so I showed the fifteen people who braved the rain how divining rods worked in the street and in the Priory graveyard. During the demonstration, I told them the story above but said that there was no way of proving the theory. However I did notice that some of the graves had one occupant, so I set them to each find a single occupancy and I would approach it from the non-lettered side of the gravestone and ask the two questions above. Fortunately, I was correct every time.

It also worked for most when I gave them rods to repeat the experiment. There was one gentleman who was quite convinced it was pure chance, coincidence or 'mumbo-jumbo' and tried six times to prove his point. He got the correct answer each time but still went away unconvinced. I have always found that people believe what they want to believe.

CHAPTER THREE
The Pre-Roman Ages

Humans are known to have been in the area now known as the Borders since about 8,000 BC The Middle Stone Age (Mesolithic) lasted from about then until c 4,000 BC and the New Stone Age (Neolithic) from c 4,000 BC to c 2000 BC These figures are educated guesswork and may be wrong by as much as 1,000 years. Carbon dating and pollen analysis give a more accurate dating when available.

The evidence of people living in the area depends on the concentrations of flint tools and waste material which can be found all over the Borders but mostly along the banks of the Tweed and its tributaries. There are well over a hundred known sites and there will be many more as yet unfound. That human existence in the Borders between 8,000 BC and 2,000 BC is known, is thanks to a few dedicated field-walkers who plodded through the fields every winter to retrieve the small chips of flint and chert which get turned up by the plough. Sadly, many of their collections get thrown out on their death or are donated to local museums where they lie unseen in stores.

But it is through the field-walkers' collections that we know anything about the families of hunter-gatherers who lived on what they could trap or collect from the forest floor. They were regarded as having highly mobile lives, living on one spot until the immediate food supply ran out and then moving on to fresh ground. However, the large number of flint tools and waste chips found on certain locations, suggest that they had a main camp usually at a river junction together with a network of outlying temporary sites.

There is enough evidence to state that the main camp was a permanent settlement, probably to house the old, the young, pregnant mothers and for over-wintering. This meant that substantial buildings would be constructed on the site. At Howick in Northumberland, a circular sunken-floored building with postholes for timbers that would have supported a conical roof was excavated and found to date to around

7,800 BC through carbon dating. It was 6 metres in diameter and could house six to eight people. A similar one at East Barnes near Dunbar, was of similar construction but oval and measuring 5metres by 5.8metres. This was dated to around 8,000 BC.

Fieldwalkers have established that there were concentrations of Mesolithic and Neolithic flint, chert and stone tools at The Rink in Selkirkshire, Dryburgh Mains in Berwickshire and Springwood Park and Kalemouth in Roxburghshire. Using divining rods, I have found patterns of postholes to confirm that buildings similar to those of Howick and East Barnes could be found in those sites. However, excavation would be required to prove that; and excavation is expensive. (This will be a familiar refrain through the book.)

THE RINK

I will take The Rink as a specimen site because it is only three miles from my home and it was the place that I served my apprenticeship as a field-walker.

Twenty years ago I gave up for study a collection of 9,600 pieces of chert, flint and stone tools with associated waste flakes/chips that I had picked up from the ploughed fields on a glacial terrace at The Rink Farm, the site where the Tweed and Ettrick Rivers meet. As I was only one of four field-walkers who regularly walked the site and their collections would be at least equal to mine, about 40,000 pieces of man-struck pieces of hard stone have been found on the site with many more still there to be found.

The Rink was a good site, a glacial deposit containing many natural chert nodules and well-placed on the higher ground above the river banks. Chert does not work as easily as flint but was a good local substitute and was used for most of the tools and waste found there. With such attractions, it had been a well-used meeting place for a period of several thousand years to judge by the tool types found.

The main concentration is in the triangular field at **NT 488 324**. Divining rods indicate circles of postholes that would once have been wooden houses, and these usually coincide with flint concentrations. In size, the houses vary from 4.5 metres to 6 metres in diameter. Considering that all organic material of wood, bone, sinew and hide has long vanished and only chert, flint and stone implements have survived, we can still tell much from the lithic assemblage. The tool types are mostly Mesolithic and made from local grey, green and black chert but there were specimens of grey and yellow flint from Yorkshire, tuff from Cumbria, red jasper from Dirleton, East Lothian, Bowmont Water agate and a few pieces of pitchstone from Arran. The early settlers at The Rink were either long-distance travellers or there was an established trading route throughout the country from the earliest days of human occupation.

The tool types indicated a hunting and gathering economy – the tiny battered-back microliths for arrowpoints and barbs, larger rounded scrapers for dressing fat from skins, knife flakes which retain their sharpness from thousands of years before, sharp points for piercing and boring. There were stones chipped into figure 8s, the large ones used as net sinkers for fishing in the nearby river and the small ones for a bolas-type weapon. From these, we have some ideas about their hunting activities, the gatherers who collected plants and nuts have left little trace.

The site around the field at **NT 488 324** has produced very few pieces that are definitely Neolithic but there may be an explanation for this.

On The Rink Farm at **NT 48912 32853**, there is a glacial mound that shows three faint concentric rings round the top. This showed up best in the drought conditions of 1959 when most of the Borders had turned beige. These rings are neither natural nor made by animals trotting round in circles. Many years later, when investigated by divining rods, it was found that there were four concentric rings of postholes round the flattish top which had a posthole in the middle. This central area had a diameter of around ten metres.

Working out all the probabilities, I came to the conclusion that it was likely to be a house on the high central area with two or three lean-to extensions built round it to be used for storage or animal sheds as and when required. These additions were about 2.3 metres in width. The whole is likely to have been roofed and thatched. By building on a sandy mound, drainage was no problem and heat from animals in the lower enclosures would rise to provide a warm if smelly atmosphere for the human living quarters during the winter.

Mound House at Rink Farm

On searching for evidence in air photographs* of the site, I found that the bottom of the mound had three ditch marks round it and one leading out to enclose some land in the vicinity. These were about 30cms in width and were likely to have been a post-palisade enclosing the site. There were three distinct phases of construction as the ditches are in different tracks.

* Google Maps are a great boon to the earthbound amateur archaeologist.

The idea of a large house on a mound is not so stupid a suggestion as it might seem because I did not work the theory out until I had investigated many similar mounds across the Borders. Not all glacial mounds had been built on but enough had to convince me that I was on the right track.

On The Rink farm, further examples of similar 'mound houses' can be found at **NT 48689 32895, NT 48733 32946** and **NT 48930 32908**. Opposite the farm cottages at **NT 48130 32097**, is another mound house with a palisaded field enclosing about an acre beside it. On this one, Mrs Caroline Cruickshank found a portion of a jet armlet which is now in the National Museum.

Transferring the search for similar structures, I went to Linglie Farm near Selkirk where I had noticed similar ring-markings on the fluvio-glacial mounds there and found three definites and one probable. The definites are at **NT 46662 29664** which has three rings and is 8m across, **NT 45722 29772, NT 47003 29660** and the probable at **NT 47127 29680**.

There are also some graves at **NT 47003 29660** within a palisaded enclosure.

On a field at **Kalemouth NT 714 277,** there was sandy knowe which was ploughed in the 1960s. This produced a good number of finer quality tools of flint, agate, jasper and pitchstone together with two sherds of pottery, one of which had been gritted with an earlier pottery. This was definitely a Neolithic settlement.

By using divining rods over the site, I found four concentric rings of postholes indicating a house similar to the one on The Rink. This is another example of a 'mound house' and there are at least three others in the near vicinity, but I gave up then as I reckoned that four was a good sample.

Springwood Park, Kelso. NT 720 333. This area at the junction of the Tweed and the Teviot is literally covered with finds from all ages from Mesolithic to Medieval. Field-walkers have been able to pinpoint flint-chipping concentrations and on these, divining rods indicate so many postholes that it is nearly impossible to tell where one hut finishes and another starts.

However, Springwood Park has items which the other flint sites lack – it has two henge monuments on a promontory at the east end of the field above the Showground.

Henges are Neolithic religious monuments, roughly circular in shape with a ditch and upcast bank but, unlike defensive structures, the bank is on the outside of the ditch.

There were rings of large timber posts within the structure. The one certain example of this type of monument in the Borders, is at Overhowden near Oxton but there may be others at Sprouston, Mellerstain and Ancrum. There are probably many more waiting discovery but wood deterioration and centuries of ploughing has left no surface trace. This is where divining rods come in useful.

I have known about the two henges at Springwood since the 1970s when I was doing a lot of field-walking on this prolific site and had noted that few flint tools could be found on the promontory. I decided that this could be a henge monument for no other reason than 'a feeling' but never felt the need to prove my assumption until now.

In fact, there were two henges on the same promontory, both quite alike in construction but of different sizes. Both had two rings of internal posts, the outer ring was 5 metre spacings and the inner at 4 metre. The entrances were facing north-east. The larger at **NT 72298 33274** was c 32m across between the ditches and the other at **NT 72361 33280** was c 27m across. Despite the similarity, it is unlikely that they would be contemporary.

Of course nothing can be proved without excavation or an improved method of geophysics, but this gives the place to look.

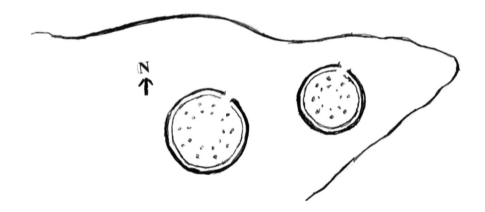

Henge Monuments at Springwood Park, Kelso

Dryburgh Mains, NT 588 326. This is a site where Mesolithic and Neolithic tools and waste are found in the river haughs there in quantity. I have never tried divining rods on this site but barbed and tanged arrowheads of the Neolithic to Bronze Age are not uncommon.

The flint sites of the Borders are numerous and would require a great deal of study before the thousand of years of the flint ages could be fitted into a time scale. This is unlikely to happen.

FORTS AND SETTLEMENTS

Most of the hill forts of the pre-Roman era are recorded in the Inventories of the Border Counties. The reason for this is that they are clearly visible. Little work has been done on excavating and a tentative dating is given as making their first appearance around 500 BC and continuing until the Early Historic period c 1000 AD. This is guesswork rather than proof positive.

I know of two hillforts in Selkirkshire which are not recorded. One is on Fairnilee Hill where a hillfort with seven or eight scooped huts and an associated field system at **NT 460 337**, was observed in the snow. The second is at Broadmeadows in the Yarrow Valley, where a hillfort with terraces around it was observed at **NT 416 307**. This one I am not so sure about.

Settlements with a palisade enclosure are less obvious as there are usually no visible traces on the ground. For them, being at the right place at the right time is handy and here divining rods come into their own.

Synton Mossend. South of the drained moss at **NT 485 204,** there is a palisade enclosure, the palisade of which can be seen in very dry summers. Checking with divining rods showed several round hut-circles approx 10 metres in diameter. These may be associated with the earthwork at Ashkirkshiel, No 137 on the Inventory of Selkirkshire, in which it is described as '*probably a medieval or later farmstead*'.

In the late 1960s when we (the Cruickshanks and I) were testing the use of divining rods as an archaeological aid, we were given permission to dig trial pits on this monument. In the first metre square, some lumps of what seemed to be inch-thick concrete came up and were put aside. This was followed another rounded piece of concrete with a bronze dagger guard and an iron blade stuck inside. This made us re-assess the finds and join the pieces together to form a rough pot. I have to admit that this was a lucky find but the National Museum was quite happy to accept the Iron Age pottery and metal pieces. One learned academic pronounced that the dagger guard could be dated to 50 B.C.

Near Synton Mossend, a metal-detectorist found a hoard of 225 Roman coins on a most unlikely location. On investigating the site with a specialist from the National Museum, I discovered that there was a hut-circle near the find-spot and this was inside a ditched and palisaded enclosure. There were two similar ones nearby, one of which contained a burial mound.

Eldinhope, Yarrow. At **NT 297 239** there is a large palisaded enclosure with twenty or more divined hut circles. This is unrecorded but many of the flint items in the collection of Tom Scott, the local artist and collector, came from this site. They were mostly fine Neolithic and Bronze Age tools.

CAIRNS

Cairns are much easier to find even when all the stones have been removed for dykes during the agricultural changes of the 1700s/1800s.

I have detailed most of the tumuli/cairns of Selkirkshire Book One. Those were at Eldinhope, Sundhope and Dryhope in the Yarrow Valley together with The Shaws, Elibank, Galashiels and Essenside in the rest of the county.

I have deliberately missed out the complex site of Whitehope/Whitefield which is a 'Valley of the Tombs' in the Yarrow Valley, as it is a complex site which will need a lot of studying.

There are other sites like at **Easter Housebyres** where remains of a round cairn can be seen at **NT 543 382** at the edge of a partly drained loch. Divining rods suggest a round cairn with an internal chamber 3 metres square, with an entrance from the east.

Whitslaid Hill, NT 4323 187. Beside the line of a minor Roman road leading from the east/west road from Craik to Tweedmouth, and the fort at Oakwood, there are several round barrows similar to those that appear in the adjacent parish of Roberton.

Sunderland Hall, NT 481 319. The remains of a long cairn can be seen under the trees about 50 yards to the east of the Hall. Divining rods suggest a 2m x 0.80m grave at the eastern end.

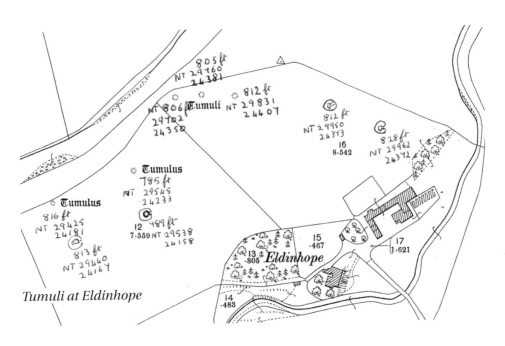

Tumuli at Eldinhope

OLD MELROSE

The field at the end of the promontory of Old Melrose is literally covered with the post holes of circular buildings. They vary in diameter from 9m upwards to 24m and most have two or more rings of post holes although there is one with six rings which must be over 30m across. In September 2011, I was taking a party of fifty on a conducted tour round the site and persuaded them to stand on the places where posts once stood. The living 'posts' made a convincing pattern for a large circular building but there were not enough of them to stand in for each post. This was a big circular building.

I first noticed the circular buildings while looking at the 1983 air photographs of the site where they appear as faint but discernable marks. On divining the area, I could match reality to the marks but found a lot more of what seemed to be circular houses which could fit into any age between Bronze and Early Historic. Many seemed to have four opposed entrances, 2m wide and there were circular rings of graves pointing inwardly to the centre. I gave up on these at the time – and still do as this really is a job for experts.

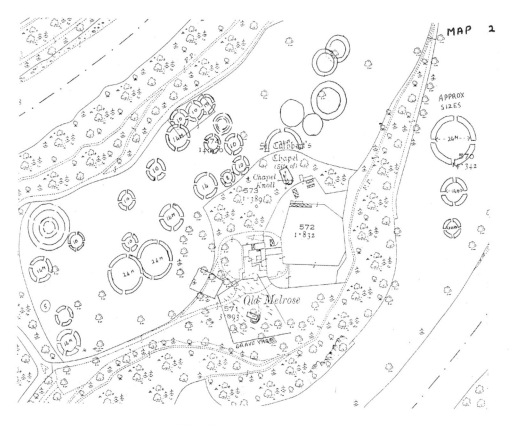

Hut Circles at Old Melrose

CHAPTER FOUR

The Roman Era

In the later part of the 1st Century, the Romans arrived in what is now the Scottish Borders. They came with a well organised army which left its mark on the landscape in the shape of permanent forts, fortlets, roads and temporary camps where marching armies rested for a night.

Although they came as conquerors, they did not seem to have left many garrisons to secure their newly-gained land. Of the six proven forts in the region, only Trimontium was occupied during the period of Roman rule which is reckoned to be between AD 80 and AD 180. Even then, it was periodically deserted when troops were withdrawn back to the line of Hadrian's Wall or posted to other parts of the Empire. The small fort at Cappuck may have come within these dates but opinion is divided on this.

Oakwood and Easter Happrew were occupied from about AD 80–100, while Lyne and probably Oxton were reckoned to be in the Antonine period, AD 142–158. With three of these forts on the line of Dere Street and two on the east/west roads, this left Oakwood as a sole stand-alone fort. Obviously there were more still to be found and the best place to look for them was along the line of the roads.

It was on the road-lines that most of the known temporary camps in the area were found by Professor St Joseph of Cambridge University who, for his development of this science, became known as the father of Air Archaeology. Since then, later generations of air-photographers have been revealed many more.

When a Roman force marched into a new area, they built a temporary defensive structure each night to give a measure of security to the sleeping troops. This was usually a low bank of earth with a ditch in front. As these camps were often occupied for one night only, they have left little trace of their being on the modern field surface after two thousand years of agriculture. It is only in the unploughed ground in the hills that they can be seen in anything like their original state.

Air photography has allowed archaeologists to pick up the crop marks of these temporary camps. Most are squarish or the standard playing-card shape with a single mound and ditch, straight sides and rounded corners. An open gateway in the middle of each wall was given some protection by a length of mound and ditch in front of it. There were variations in the size and design of the camps constructed by individual legions and a chain of similar sized camps allow us to trace the progress of different sizes of Roman units through the country.

Inside the camp were rows of tents housing the troops. According to the Roman military manuals, each messing unit of eight men shared a leather tent that measured 3 metres by 3 metres and beside each, a hole was dug for rubbish. When the troops moved on these pits were filled in as part of the tiding-up process. This left soil-disturbances that were the equivalent of postholes, and thus detectable by divining rods. This was to prove very useful in finding temporary camps that had left no visible trace on the surface.

By walking with divining rods over known temporary camps, I was able to determine that the rubbish pits were in rows that were about 8 metres from each other and that individual pits in the row were 6 metres apart. By conclusion, I reckoned that each eight-man tent stood on a 48 square metres of ground. Further to that, I was able to work out the position of the tent by finding where its four corner tent-poles which had been dug into the ground. By locating on which side a further two tent-poles were placed, I could tell the position of the door and which way the tent faced.

After inspecting several camps, I realised that the tents did not uniformly face in one direction but had their door flap facing towards the nearest gateway. These would be placed for a quick response to attack.

Taking this as a standard, I could look for temporary camps on potentially promising positions but which showed had no visible remains in air photographs.

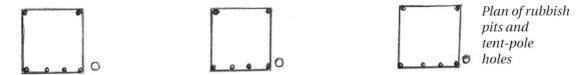

Plan of rubbish pits and tent-pole holes

One thing I did pick up fairly quickly was that the Roman army tended to have favoured places which they returned to many times. So if there is proof of one marching camp on a site, there are likely to be more in the vicinity. If the same site is used many times and rows of tents, post-holes, mound and ditches intermingle, this makes life difficult for the diviner.

However not all of the recorded temporary camps have these distinctive markings. Some have lines of what can only be permanent or semi-permanent buildings varying in size from 10 to 15m in length and consistently 4/4.5m across. Some show no signs of tents or buildings and these were probably field enclosures because Roman armies travelled with many animals in their baggage trains. One enclosure on the side of Dere Street at Pennymuir is likely to have been a waggon park. I will return to this subject in more detail later.

FIRST CLAIMS

The first record of a Roman presence in Scotland was written by the Roman historian and politician Publius Cornelius Tacitus. His father-in-law, Gnaeus Julius Agricola, was governor of the province of Brittania from AD 77 (or 78) to AD 83. In an attempt to increase his own and his father-in-law's political stature, Tacitus wrote *'de vita Agricolae'* claiming that Agricola had defeated and colonised the wild area to the north of the Province of Brittania and had brought it under Roman rule by establishing a network of roads and building forts on sites that he had chosen. Military successes were an asset to those who sought senatorial office but like most political claims, 'de vita Agricolae' must be viewed with some caution.

Yet it is the only written record we have and generations of archaeologists accepted the information contained in the book as the literal truth and something to confirm their own beliefs. This led to the accepted truth that Agricola was the first governor to lead a Roman army into what is now Scotland in AD 79/80 and was the first to establish a Roman fort at Trimontium near Newstead. The site was well-chosen on a natural mound overlooking the River Tweed and at a crossroads where the north/south traffic intersected with the east/west movement along the river bank.

This fort was to eventually become the centre of Roman occupation in the eastern Borders, varying in purpose from a military outpost to a supply centre and finishing as stronghold for the retreating army. Of this, more later.

Agricola's claims are now being questioned. It is postulated that the first forays into the area were under the governorship of Q Petillius Cerialis and happened between AD 71 and AD 74. Pottery, glass and a large proportion of coins from the pre-Agricolan period are not uncommon in the forts of southern Scotland and as far as the line of what was later known as the Antonine Wall. Carlisle was long claimed to be an Agricolan foundation but dendrochronology (ring-growths in wood) has proved that the first permanent fort there was established in late AD 72.

In Selkirkshire Book One, I gave the opinion that *'with a line of forts established between the Tyne and Solway, it would be most unusual if no reconnaissance was made in strength to the north of the line. The site at Newstead is at a convenient crossroads and ideal for an occasionally used temporary camp'*. This was my first conjectural period of occupation of the fort.

From many years of field-walking and divining the site, I knew that the first permanent fort lay within an enclosure which suggested a temporary or marching camp. On the east side of the fort, there was a rampart and ditch which does not fit into any of the plans of the Roman defences on the site and when I mapped this out with GPS and divining rods, I got a plan that was similar to the design of camp favoured by Petillius Cerialis. This type is rectangular with three gateways on the longer sides and two on the shorter; each gateway has a titulus in front.

Although this type of temporary camp turned out to be a regular find throughout the Borders, at Trimontium it underlies the first permanent fort which makes for a date pre-AD 78.

'Cerialis' temporary camp at Trimontium

This Newstead version is approximately 440m by 230m. In the dead ground between the east wall of the first permanent fort and the east wall of the temporary camp, there are rows of rubbish pits 8 metres apart while the pits in the row are at 6m spacing with a similar pattern found in the south west corner of the camp. This is the standard pattern that I had already established in known marching camps.

The plan shown was done by field observation and divining rods. Can it be proved? Yes, by doing trial trenches in the titili or by geophysics if these have developed in the last twenty years.

THE CEREALIS TEMPORARY CAMP AT OAKWOOD

Being convinced of one Cerialis camp, I set about looking for another and found a similar shape under the Agricolan fort at Oakwood in the Ettrick valley.

This one was slightly different, being nearly square with three gateways on each side, each with a defensive titulus in front. The distance between each gateway or each gateway and the corner of the wall was sixty of my paces. On measuring my sixty paces through grass,

I found that I was covering between 34 and 37 metres. One of the standard Roman land measurement is the actus which is usually given as 35.5 metres. This is not a coincidence.

Inside the camp but outside the fort, I found the usual rubbish pits in rows 8m apart and 6m between the pits in a row. I took GPS readings at the corners of the camp (1, 5, 9 and 13) and at each gateway, remembering at the same time that GPS readings do not give pinpoint accuracy.

Two unproven temporary camps do not necessarily make for a pre-Agricolan campaign and there is the possibility that the Agricolan troops were billeted within the temporary camp while building the permanent fort within it. More evidence required.

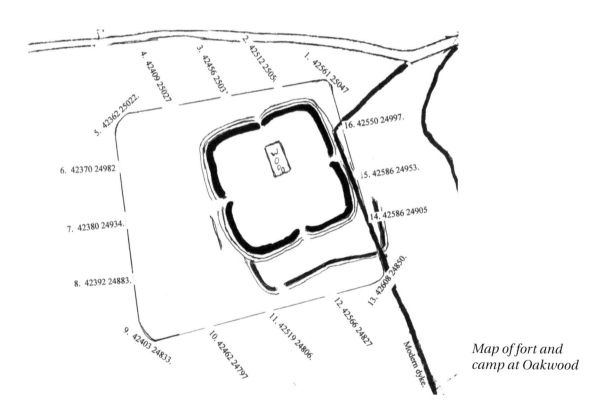

Map of fort and camp at Oakwood

CHAPTER FIVE

Trimontium

Anybody interested in the Roman occupation of the Borders starts with the fort complex of Trimontium lying to the east of the village of Newstead. The location was not always so well known for although the name appears in the 2nd century Ptolemy map of Britain where Trimontium is shown to be somewhere between Carlisle and the Antonine Wall, but because of the map's distortion the site was not known. Nor did it appear in the folklore of the Borders.

It remained lost until, in 1761 General Roy the military cartographer and antiquary, saw the three Eildon Hills and a Roman road which he called 'Watling Street' headed directly towards them. So he concluded that *'the ancient Trimontium of the Romans was situated somewhere near these remarkable hills, at the village of Eildon, Old Melros or perhaps about Newstead where the Watling Street hath passed the Tweed'.*

General Roy had a keen eye for the ground and his *'Military Antiquities of the Romans in North Britain. 1793'* gives illustrations of all known forts in Scotland at that time. Yet even his experienced eye couldn't detect any ground trace that would identify a Roman fort. With all surface traces obliterated, the great ditches filled in and the ramparts levelled, Roman Trimontium had vanished.

It was re-discovered in 1846 when pits containing Roman artefacts were found during the making of a cutting for the Border Railway. With this discovery and half a century of field finds, there was sufficient evidence for the site to be excavated by James Curle, a Melrose solicitor and amateur archaeologist, working on behalf of the Society of Antiquaries of Scotland. He supervised the excavations from 1905 to 1910 and published his findings in 1911 in *'A Roman Frontier Post and Its People'*. This provided a standard reference work for Roman studies in Britain and Europe at the time and it is still relevant to the present day.

In 1947, further excavations were carried out by Sir Ian Richmond to re-interpret some of Curle's findings. In 1987, the Bradford University Department of Archaeological Sciences did a trial dig which started a ten-year excavation of the site. The results were remarkable but still unpublished in 2012.

My own involvement with Roman Trimontium began in 1955 with some field-walking under the guidance of Bruce Mason, a Selkirk baker and keen antiquarian. Since then I have acquired a lot of knowledge of the Romans in the Borders, some from books but mostly from the ground. In Selkirkshire Book One, I used Trimontium with its many phases and finds as a template to illustrate the period and as a comparison for what was happening in the rest of the Borders.

I will use condensed versions of my text if it is relevant to the use of divining rods in archaeology and add some homemade maps and illustrations to give a better idea of where I think things are.

Nota Bene. Not everyone agrees with me.

THE FIRST ROMAN BRIDGE AT NEWSTEAD

The first permanent fort at Trimontium faces westwards, leading to the reasonable deduction that the main Roman road was on the west side of the fort. This must have come down Bank Lane, Claymires Road and Eddy Road to the flat haugh beside the river. The Inventory of Roxburghshire states that *'the topography of the S. bank clearly demands that Dere Street should have crossed the river somewhere near the existing ford at Eddy Pool'.* This may have been the site of the Rev Adam Milne's 1743 report that there was a *'famous Bridge over the Tweed; the entrance of which was very evident and many fine stones were dug out when the water was low'.*

(This location is marked as No 9 - The Site of the Roman Bridge' by Willie Alchin in his booklet on Newstead village, *'As I Recall'.*)

With this in mind, I ventured forth with my trusty divining rods to look for traces of the said bridge. I couldn't find any stone foundations but did find a double row of posts leading across the river. Although these were below the surface of the stones and gravel, the indications were that they were set in pairs 3/3.5m apart with about the same between each pair. These represent piles driven into the bed of the river to support a wooden bridge at **NT 56364 34534**. It was only after I started to think in Roman measurements in 2011 realised that they were probably the standard measure Roman measurement called a *'uncia agri'*.

Next step. If they were posts, each would have a protective iron point to prevent splitting while the pile was being driven into the river-bed. So a good metal detector might be able to get a reading there. After that, dig one out to prove the point and get wood for dating.

If there was a stone bridge on this location, I can find no trace of it. Unfortunately, the Rev. Adam Milne does not give the position of the famous bridge but it is much more likely to have been where the three modern bridges are located on the east of the Fort (Tripontium).

What happened to the *'many fine stones'* which reputedly came from the bridge in 1743? In Newstead village, there are three in old buildings and walls, which are likely to have come from Roman buildings. It is more likely that they are in the structure of the 1780's road bridge at Leaderfoot or the mansion of Drygrange; but none have been positively identified.

LOGISTICS

'Selkirkshire and the Borders – Book One' (extract, p.147)

As far as I know, the logistics of supplying the fort of Trimontium has never been considered. Taking 800 men as an average garrison, add the civilian population in the annexes to the troops out-posted at the various permanent forts in the Borders and passing units who would look to replenish their supplies as they marched along Dere Street, and the problem would be immense. It was not only food, the corn, wine and oil for rations that was required, but all the other supplies, iron, lead, leather etc needed to keep a garrison supplied.

Although Trimontium was on the edge of the Roman world, it enjoyed the benefits of the Empire. From excavation and field finds, we know that wine, oil, garum (a vile and costly sour fish sauce), currants, dates etc, sealed in large pottery jars called amphorae, came to

Trimontium from Germany, France Spain, Portugal and Italy. Tableware pottery came from all the above and as far afield as the Eastern Mediterranean. Most of this would be brought in by the traders who were established round the fort.

I made a reasonable case that a daily delivery of about 30 tonnes of supplies would be required to sustain the fort, its civilian population and hinterland garrisons. From finds of a steering oar and two boathooks, we can be fairly sure that these were brought up the Tweed to Trimontium in 'codicarae', the small punt-like boats which were each capable of carrying 10 tonnes.

I had known for some time that there were a number of long buildings in the triangular field at the south end of the above bridge. It was only while I was contemplating the logistics of supply that I put two and two together and had a closer look at the buildings there.

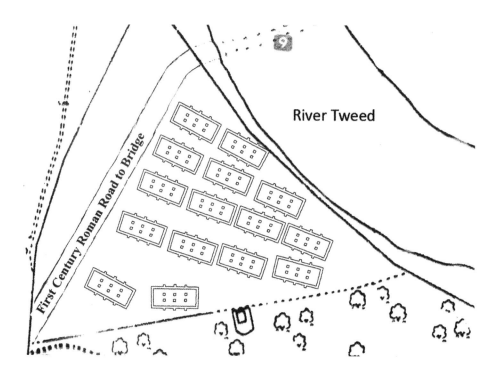

There were fifteen buildings of an almost standard size, measuring around 16 metres by 5 metres internally, with three pairs of supporting blocks at regular spacings. On the outside of the long external walls, buttresses corresponded with the supporting blocks.

These cannot be other than Roman granaries but would require excavation for proof. There may be no stones remaining and I am getting the image of 'ghost walls' but I am sticking to my granaries predictions.

As well as supplying the Trimontium and neighbouring forts, there would have to be a large supply depot from which passing troops could draw rations and other necessities. One period when a store cupboard of such dimensions would be required, was in AD 209 when the imperial army of Severus was marshaled at Trimontium before marching north to come to grips with the revolting natives. It is reckoned that their progress can be traced through the Borders in the large temporary camps at St Leonards, Channelkirk and Pathhead.

An incidental use of the Tweed as a fishing river was revealed by the discovery of a Roman bronze fish hook during excavations in the south annexe of the fort.

WATER

'Selkirkshire and the Borders – Book One' (*extract, p.147*)

I have never been convinced that all the water at Trimontium was supplied from the hundred plus pits that have been found there. The fort and its annexes must have held at least a thousand humans and their water needs, plus the requirements for the baths, could not have been supplied by surface collection. Additionally, humans need clean, drinkable water to survive and stagnant water in storage pits would not remain potable during the summer. The idea that enough water could have been supplied from a subterranean water table is not feasible.

The obvious source was from the foot of the Eildons where many natural springs are to be found. I traced a drainage line from there to what can only be a header tank measuring 11m by 7m at **NT 56843 33898**. *From there the line went straight downhill towards the west side of the fort. To carry across the dip on the south of the fort, the water passed through 8cm sealed* *pipes, fragments of which I find along that line.* Just after it crossed the Melrose Bypass, a branch pipe came off the main supply pipe and went to a large building which turned out to be the second baths which everybody reckoned had to be somewhere around but nobody was prepared to speculate where it was likely to be. A closer look at the site found another branch from the pipe leading off to the west. This went to a latrine on the north of the bathhouse.

As water, bathhouses and latrines are closely connected and very important in the search for Roman forts and fortlets, I am leaving these details to a later chapter.

Before coming to the known baths, a branch pipe diverted some of the water to the houses beside the 1ˢᵗ century road in the South Annexe. These pipes are much smaller in diameter.

Archaeologist James Curle reports that *'The water pipes were of two kinds – the larger fifteen and a half inches in length, with a diameter of three inches, neatly made with faucet joints having a diameter of one inch and three-quarters, the smaller without faucets and with a diameter of one inch. The latter probably served as branch pipes'.*

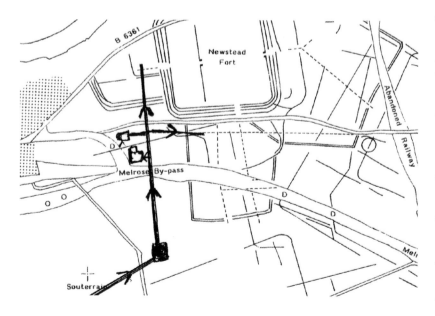

At a guess, some of the pits in the South Annexe may have been wells but it is more likely that they were water storers rather than water collectors. It is probable that most would simply be soak-away pits for waste water, urine etc.

Fort with header tank and line of pipes

ALTARS

In '*A Roman Frontier Post and Its People*', James Curle notes that '*the comparative absence of inscribed stones was a disappointing feature of the excavations*'. He published the six altars which had been found on the site, the first in 1783. Of the six, four were found in the southern part of the East Annexe.

As a fieldwalker, I walked this area many times but gradually ignored one part of it because there was little to be found on the surface there. It eventually dawned on me that this was the obvious place for the parade ground, beside the fort and reasonably flat.

Romans took their parade ground very seriously, having animal sacrifices at the beginning of each year and, according to one theory, burying the previous year's altars round the edge of the parade ground; this latter is unproven although much repeated.

My own theory, equally unproven, was that the altars were placed round the parade ground and left standing there to show that this was a sacred place, guarded against intruders by the Roman gods. This could be a Roman duplication of the 'head walls' set up to protect the Celtic forts and holy places. My idea is that the altars would only be buried when the fort was being evacuated or when one garrison unit was replaced with another. As I say, unproven but logical.

The first altar from the East Annexe was found in 1783 and was dedicated to the 'Campestres', the Gods of the Parade Ground, by a cavalry decurion. Remembering that another three of the previously excavated altars were found on the same approximate line of ditch,

to see if there were any others to be found, I walked the ditch of the East Annexe with divining rods. With a GPS, I noted the locations where these are to be found and hope that some day, someone might believe my findings enough to conduct a trial excavation. Even better would

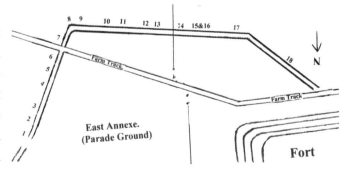

be to excavate the whole lot because there is a lot of information on the stones telling which units were garrisoned in the fort during the occupation.

Starting at the East Gate of the East Annexe, altars are located at:

1.	**NT 57336 34355**	2.	**NT 57336 34339**	3.	**NT 57342 34321**
4.	**NT 57345 34308**	5.	**NT 57347 34293**	6.	**NT 57345 34279**
7.	**NT 57339 34268**	8.	**NT 57332 34255**	9.	**NT 57308 34224**
10.	**NT 57304 34213**	11.	**NT57299 34202**	12.	**NT 57289 34203**
13.	**NT 57277 34206**	14.	**NT 57249 34211**	15 & 16	**NT57163 34226**
17.	**NT 57153 34232**	18.	**NT 57125 34273**		

All the altars are lying along the line of the ditch and in the middle of it except for No 14 which is lying across the ditch. Excavation required to prove/disprove.

TEMPLES

Still on the subject of religion, there are two probable Roman temples, both lying outside the fort complex on Eildon Mains Farm. One at **NT 57605 33683** is a nearly square shape 11m by 10.5m with a smaller 6m square joined on to it. The other at **NT 57003 33788** is L-shaped with three rooms each approximately 7m by 7m. Both have walls approximately 1m thick and the stones are still in place, these structures could be easily located by geo-physics.

GRAVEYARD, NT57070 34087

During the Bradford excavations south of the bypass, but still within the south annexe, several shallow scoops were found below the plough-disturbed soil. At the time, these were reckoned to be animal feeding places as they were within wicker-fence enclosures. However, one of the scoops was deeper than the others and this was found to contain burnt bones (probably human), Roman pottery, carbon deposits and, most importantly, thirteen white quartz pebbles with one highly polished face. These have been recognised as the 'ball-bearings' of a Roman cart, inserted into the wooden axle or wheel to minimise wear on the wood. So there was little doubt that this was a cremation deposit although we will have to wait for the Bradford publication to confirm that.

Using divining rods (2012), I found that the graveyard is approximately 50m by 15m and contains 13 rows of pits with at least six pits per row. There probably would be more as the rows stop at the edge of the cutting.

THE HORSES OF TRIMONTIUM

This is more a practical countryman's comment than that of a diviner but I think this is an aspect of Roman Trimontium that is badly neglected.

In 'A Roman Frontier Post and its People', James Curle notes that *'among the domestic animals, the most notable was the horse'*. When bones of horses from that excavation were analysed, they were found to vary in height from 11 to 16 hands but the majority were around 14 hands with some fine-boned animals of Libyan and Arab descent and evidence of cross-breeding . (Curle Appendix II).

During the Bradford Excavations in 1987/97, horse skulls and bones came out of the pits and ditches frequently and many of the finds from excavations and field-walking are horse related. So we can safely say that there were a lot of horses at Trimontium in its phases of occupation.

It is difficult to state what proportion of legionary, auxiliary and cavalry troops were billeted in the fort at any one time. From altar evidence, we know that vexillations of the Twentieth Legion and the Ala Vocontiorum, a cavalry unit, were in the garrison during the 2nd century occupation of the fort. Other than that, we must make reasoned deductions based on the available evidence.

While looking at air photographs of the site, I have long noted a large circular mark in the middle of the East Annexe at **NT 57309 34414**. It is not usual to get circular marks in a Roman camp complex and this one seems to have been unseen or ignored. Divining rods suggest a solid circular palisade enclosing an area about 30m in diameter and another outer ring of posts set 2m from the first. This is almost identical to a similar structure at Lunt that was interpreted as a gyrus, a training pen for cavalry horses and recruits. This would fit in with the altar of the decurion of the Ala Augusta of the Vocontiorum which was found nearby. Horses were important in an outpost fort and they had to be kept fit. In one of the last phases of occupation, the principia building was replaced by a larger roofed hall which is thought to have been used to exercise the cavalry horses during the winter.

THE CAVALRY UNIT

The Roman cavalry unit was the *'Ala Quingenaria'* a unit of 500 men in theory. The larger unit was the *'Ala Milliaria'*, an implied unit of 1000 men – it usually hovered around 768. Then there was the 'Cohors Quingenaira Equitata' a mixed unit of 480 light infantry and 128 cavalry. The Roman cavalry horse was a mare or gelding around 14 hands high. Its average service life was four to five years. The mares were never bred from at this stage, as the breeding/rearing cycle would take three years from their service life.

It has been estimated that each horse would need about 2kgs of the barley that was grown at that period and 5kgs of hay daily if kept in a stable and two acres of good grazing or four acres of rough grazing if out to pasture. Thus each horse would require about four acres of good land to graze and to grow barley and hay for its active survival. Most of this would come from the neighbouring countryside. Evidently the Roman troops supplied their own as scythes for cutting hay and sickles for barley and oats were found in the Trimontium pits.

If we take 128 men as the standard number of cavalry at Trimontium – and this is a very low figure for such an important fort – they would require around 160 horses for mounts and re-mounts. Added to that would be another 40 for the unit's pack/haulage purposes, so we would be looking for a minimum of 800 acres to graze and supply the fodder for the Trimontium horses of this small unit alone.

In Curle's excavations, it was noted that the First Century pits contained strong evidence of a cavalry force in the shape of parade helmets, horse accoutrements, horse skulls etc. The Second Century showed a similar dependence on horse power when the fort was rebuilt several times with the main entrance from the south or east.

In the fifth phase c 140–158 AD, a reducing/dividing wall was built within the fort. It has been proposed that this was built to separate a detachment of the Twentieth Legion from the Ala Augusta Vocontiorum, both of whom can be proved to garrison Trimontium in the Antonine period. The theory is that the smaller section contained eight barrack/stable blocks to house the 512 cavalrymen of the Ala Vocontiorum. However this theory is hypothetical rather than confirmed by excavation.

Shortly after AD 160, another massive change took place. The Antonine Wall was abandoned and Trimontium became a frontier outpost again. Within the fort, the internal wall was demolished and the legionary barracks were rebuilt as barrack/stable blocks. In front of the headquarters building, a large hall, 150 feet long and 50 feet wide, may have been an in-door riding school for exercising the cavalry horses. In this phase, Trimontium seems to have been garrisoned by an Ala Milliaria, 768 cavalrymen with probably 1000 horses. The most likely candidate is the Ala Petriana which had been stationed at Corbridge and Stanwick near Carlisle previously. This would provide a Rapid-Reaction Force to give advance warning of any hostile approach. In logistic terms, this unit would require yearly fodder of 635 tonnes of barley, roughly the same weight of hay for the winter and a minimum of 2000 acres of good grazing land for summer consumption.

For the Romans, the land around the fort was ideal for a cavalry unit. The Eildon Hills and Bowden Common would make excellent training grounds while the flatter land around the fort could provide fodder for the horses. The Annay lands between Newstead and Melrose seems to have been divided up into fields about 100 metres square with paths between. Equally likely are flat lands of Gattonside Haugh and Dryburgh Mains which have produced Roman coins. Taken together as hay meadows, these would provide enough land for the hay supply; it could then be used for autumn and early winter grazing.

One problem is in identifying the field systems around the fort; eighteen hundred years of subsequent agricultural use has obliterated most of the traces. On looking at the air photos of the site, it is apparent that several of the ditch lines marked as 'Roman Temporary Camp' are unlikely to be that, as the steepness of the ground would make pitching tents impractical, and these are more likely to have been enclosed for grazing. However a short-term temporary camp would make ideal field enclosures after the troops had left.

Additionally, there are several ditched enclosures away from the fort which have been un-noticed or ignored. These do not show the rubbish pit/tent marks of a temporary camp.

Roman finds suggests that the area from Maxton to Melrose and Bowden to Dryburgh was used to supply the base at Trimontium. A large Roman fort with its requirements, would present a great trading opportunity for local entrepreneurs and it is interesting to note that the native settlement at Lilliesleaf, 10kms from the fort, had a spread of Roman objects very similar to that in the south annexe of 2nd century Trimontium.

'EARTH HOUSES' AT NEWSTEAD

In the spring of 1845, a man was cutting a drain from a spring in one of the fields south of Newstead village when he struck what seemed to be an underground tunnel. This caused some sensation and was visited by curious neighbours, none of whom could give any explanation as to its age or function. One of the onlookers was the architect, John Smith of Darnick, who drew a plan and noted details of the structure.

'The building was rather more than two feet under the surface of the ground and consisted of two low, apparently sunk or face walls about three feet deep, built of hewn stone (reddish sandstone) laid in courses, and inclosing an elongated space, increasing gradually in breadth from the opening to the other extremity, which was shut in by a semicircular wall; the whole forming, from being bent considerably, a figure somewhat resembling a chemist's retort. The walls were formed of only one stone in thickness and each stone is described as varying from about six to ten or twelve inches in depth; they seem to have been built dry as no appearance of lime or mortar was observed. The entrance or doorway was turned towards the north-west, and was four feet two inches in width; seventeen feet from this, the building was five feet four inches wide; eighteen feet further up the interior, it was six feet nine inches; and eighteen feet still further, it was seven feet in width; the whole length of the interior, measured across the centre, being fifty-four feet; and a line drawn from the outside across to the beginning of the curved extremity was thirty-six feet in length. Nothing was found within the space enclosed by the walls of the building, except for dressed stones of various sizes and shapes; some of them simply flat pavement-like slabs, which were most numerous near the entrances; others, flat stones bevelled on one side, along which a notch was cut longitudinally. These last were about seven and a half inches thick, the bevelled projection being seven inches in length; they were indiscriminately mixed with the pavement-like

stones which were about the same thickness; but the bevelled stones were found in the wider portions of the interior or from the middle to the closed extremity. Two larger stones were also found, having rich moulding cut on one side.'

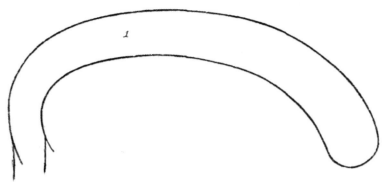

John Smith's 'Earth House'

In P.S.A.S. 1852, Dr J.A. Smith, Secretary to the Society of Antiquaries, notes that *'Another ruin, said to be of a somewhat similar kind was found in the adjoining field in the spring of 1849, about a hundred yards to the east of the building mentioned. It is described as having resembled the other considerably, except that it was built of whinstone as well as sandstone and the stones were not so neatly dressed, being altogether of a rougher character. The materials of which were dug out for economical purpose and after following it for some ten or twelve feet, further progress was arrested by its passing under an adjoining road which formed the boundary of the man's field, and consequently put a final conclusion to his operations.'*

After comparisons with other structures and a suggestion that they were likely to have been connected with the secret rites of a native priesthood, Dr Smith notes that *'several coins of Constantine the Great were stated to have been found in the immediate vicinity.'*

It was after twenty-five years of field-walking the main fort and annexes of Trimontium that I decided to have a look at the field where 'Earth House' was marked with a cross.

Field-walking produced nothing, not even a scrap of pottery, but divining rods showed a series of peculiar shapes. The suggested shape was a long path with a big round blob at the end; rather like the bottom half of a golf club (a driver) or the top half of a musical minim, but on a much larger scale, these being about sixteen metres in length.

Even although the shapes were unlike the 'chemist's retort' of John Smith, I thought they might be of interest to archaeological researchers, so I drew them out as a plan and sent these to several archaeologists but got no response.

Another twenty-five years later, none the wiser but now more experienced, I got two metal-detectorists to try the field when it was ploughed in the spring of 2011. They got nothing either but I got a lot more 'golf club' shapes and they were in regimented rows. I did note that the bulbous end was always facing uphill. Taking more time, I found that each one intruded into a rectangular shape enclosed by a wall 0.8 metre thick and measuring about 8 metres by 4 metres internally. These were obviously houses and the 'golf clubs', far from being earth houses themselves, were storage space for food.

Being nearly two metres into the ground according to John Smith, they were the equivalent of the root cellars in the American mid-west before the days of refrigeration. They provided a low temperature and steady humidity, keeping food from freezing in winter and cool in the summer months. In all, I stepped out about eighty to make sure of uniformity. They were in four rows or rather two streets because the houses were aligned facing each other and about six metres apart. There were others in the field but eighty was a fair sample. I was slightly bothered that none of them gave the retort shape that the Darnick architect had noted and also that there was no Roman pottery found in the field.

It was only when I went into Field B that the retort shapes appeared. This field was on a slope running down the village and a sixteen metre tunnel into the slope would require much more digging. So to counter this, the builders made the tunnel to fit the curve of the slope. In Field B, I checked out twelve locations and found the same size of building had a retort shape on the higher side. Here the buildings were over twenty metres apart because the retort shape extended beyond the house.

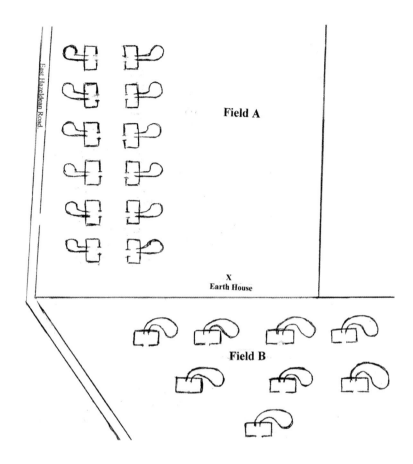

While doing this, I remembered noting that a number of dark patches appear in this field when it was ploughed. As dark patches are always worth investigating, I had gone over to discover that they were household rubbish middens from Georgian and Victorian days but it was unusual to find them in the middle of an arable field. It is only recently that I realised that they must have been infilling for existing holes.

John Smith's description of a seven foot bulb at the end of the tunnel could not have been spanned by a stone covering. So the roof support would have to be wood which rots with age, causing the roof to collapse and leave a hole to be filled with Georgian rubbish etc.

On passing divining rods over the sites, they showed the retort shape of a root cellar/ earth house. Additionally, several of these are now growing clumps of thistles which are deep-rooting plants.

Could the earth-houses/root cellars be proved? Quite easily by excavation as the household debris and ashes would be very different to the 3rd/4th century constructions. Taking a wider picture, the location of a planned settlement near a deserted fort is quite consistent with a society that had been romanised for four or five generations; it is just that the concept has never been suggested for southern Scotland.

To Dr Smith's note on the coins of Constantine found in the vicinity, can be added two coin moulds from south of the fort. These have been described as being used for making forgeries but I put forward the suggestion that they were being made as the local variant of the Roman currency which was now not being brought into Scotland by the army. This did not meet with much approval but sense might yet prevail.

Strangely, no Roman Samian pottery has been picked up from the site despite its close proximity to Trimontium. This may infer that the settlement if such it be, belongs to the period after about AD 250 when few pieces of Samian were appearing north of Hadrian's Wall.

CHAPTER SIX

Roman Bathhouses in the Borders

I am taking this as a separate chapter because finding the bathhouse is the easiest way to locate the fort or fortlet. By following a drain taking water to a potential fort, you will come to a bathhouse or latrine which is usually inside an annexe attached to the fort. Bathhouses and latrines will appear regularly in the following chapters, not because I am a bathhouse fetishist but because I am informed that the heat-print of the bathhouse furnace should be easily traceable by geophysics and I need to convince the sceptics somehow.

TRIMONTIUM

There are only two proven, i.e., excavated, Roman bathhouses in the Scottish Borders. One is at the small fort of Cappuck **NT 213 695**, where 'a little two-roomed bathhouse' was discovered during excavations in 1886. I have doubts about this identification as I could find no drain/pipe bringing water in or taking it out.

The other is at Trimontium where James Curle's excavation revealed 'quite a small, functional building'. Many comments have been made by archaeologists that this bathhouse was too small to have provided services for the number of troops in the fort and concluded that there must have been a larger one somewhere in the vicinity. This was a logical deduction and quite acceptable – but nobody was prepared to look for it. As a reader of ground, it was obvious to me that the only place for a second baths was between the west side of the south annexe and the village of Newstead.

To hunt for it, I started with the water pipe which I already knew supplied the known baths and the south annexe, following it down to where a branch of it turned off westwards towards the village. Twenty metres along this, I found the wall of a building and spent an hour roughly drawing the structure, returning the next day to check everything because the original drawing was quite complicated.

The building lay within an enclosure in the south-west corner of the field near the junction of B6361 with A6091. This is the lowest part of the field and after nineteen centuries of soil-wash, I would not be surprised if there was a metre of earth on top of any archaeological remains. This would explain why there are no tiles, bricks and blackened soil which characterises the known baths site.

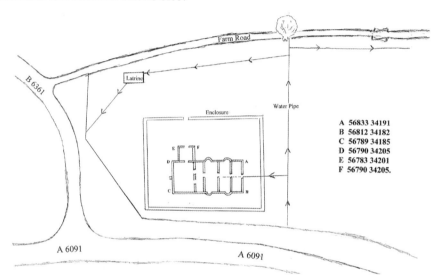

Of the building itself, the walls are about 0.7m thick. The large room nearest Newstead is the heated room with the stoke-hole on the west side and rows of hypocaust supports probably still in place – divining rods suggest 15 rows north-south and 10 rows east-west. This room is about 18m by 12m. Thereafter the picture is less clear as there seems to have been at least one reconstruction. The enclosure wall is about a metre wide and likely to have been made of stone.

N.B. The measurements given were paced along the outer edge of the walls and are approximations. Even if the measurements given are only approximately right, this is a much larger bathhouse than the known one. As a bonus during the bathhouse search, another branch pipe was discovered leading from the main pipeline. This went to a building 7m by 5m lying to the north of the bathhouse. With one water pipe going in and another leading out, this was unlikely to be anything other than a latrine. Curiously, nobody has mentioned that Curle's small latrine would not be enough to service the defecatory requirements of the garrison.

Could these baths and latrine be for the other ranks of the Roman Army or even kept for the auxiliary troops, whereas the known one was for the elite legionaries? How reliable is this? Well, these are feasible suggestions of what is there and what they are. Only the JCB, spade and trowel will give proof. However the furnace chamber which provided heat for the users also sealed the magnetic footprint of the soil around it and if I can find a friendly geophysicist, he may be able to prove (or disprove) my theory very quickly.

OTHER BATHHOUSES

Previously I never thought much about bathhouses in the Borders even though I had read that there was one attached to, or near every Roman fort. These were not just places to wash and keep clean but served the same function for leisure and recreation that the NAAFI supplied in my early soldiering days some sixty years ago. Ignoring the potential was a mistake because if I could find an unknown fort, the discovery of a bathhouse in the vicinity was an added 'proof', even if the rest of the world seemed totally uninterested.

As is mentioned below, there is a Roman fort complex at Greenlawdean in Berwickshire and the flatland beside the burn has some interesting shapes. There was one at **NT 69297 48107** which was so unusual that I made a rough drawing in my notebook and noted

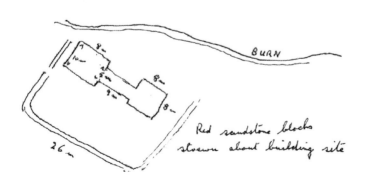

'this can only be the bathhouse for the fort at the top of the bank'. That comment was made on the slight basis that it was close to the Langrist Burn and I couldn't think what else it could possibly be.

N.B. The given measurements are for the outside of the structure.

About fifteen years later, while searching along the Roman road up Teviotdale for unrecorded Roman forts in 2011, I came across one on a flat mound at Lanton Mains. At the lower end of the field, I found a shape similar to that at Greenlawdean. It was long and narrow with walls c 0.7m thick and measured c 18m by 4m internally. It was in three sections, the ends being 4m square and joined together by a passage 9m long by 2.5m wide. The whole structure was enclosed by a wooden palisade 25m across. A drain from a low marsh in the next field led water into one of the end rooms.

So now I had two unusually long narrow buildings which I thought might be bathhouses beside two potential Roman forts. As bathhouses were kept away from other buildings to prevent the risk of fire, they usually had their own enclosure or annexe and the main body was always stone-built.

Obviously the next step was to check around known Roman forts to see if anything similar could be found. The Lyne and Oakwood forts seemed the best bets.

LYNE FORT BATHHOUSES

The search for the bathhouse/s at Lyne was spread over several months when new ideas/air photographs gave fresh slants to my views of the site. This is reflected in the extending dimensions of the fort.

The problem of bringing water into the fort had already been identified by Prof Ian Richmond in P.S.A.S. 1940-1941 with the conclusion that it must have been led along the narrow neck of land into the fort. Using divining rods for the more usual task of looking for drains, I found a header tank, about 7m square on a knowe 300m to the north of the fort and followed this down to the fort. There were three branches leaving the main aqueduct on the east side, the most southerly of which led to a long narrow bathhouse building of familiar design at **NT 18736 40743.** The aqueduct went through the fort, supplying two water-tanks and two linear bathhouses of the same shape and dimensions within the fort.

A watch tower at **NT18704 40745** was noted in passing. Both watch tower and bathhouse may have been for the use of the garrison of the nearby fortlet.

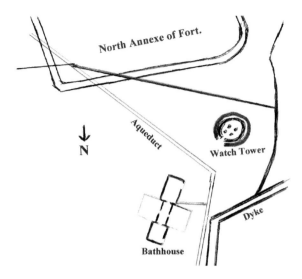

North Annexe of Fort.

↓
N

Aqueduct

Watch Tower

Dyke

Bathhouse

The long narrow building was located about 140m north of the north side of the fort and 20m east of the fortlet. It had the same three sections with broad wall-bases and two box-shaped ends and a narrow middle section. This waisted shape bothered me for several days until on another trip and closer inspection, I found that the long middle section had a door in each side leading into an 8m square room. These did not have the broad wall-base of the other rooms but seemed to be of sleeper-beam buildings.

It later became clear that this shape with variations, was the most common dimensions for a bathhouse near a Roman fort, so it seems wise to present as detailed a plan as I can, given the limitations of paced measurements.

Room A was 4m square internally with under-floor heating. In most places, the raised floor had sixteen pillars arranged in a square in the centre of the room leaving a space for seating round the base of the walls. Heat was provided by a fire under the floor.

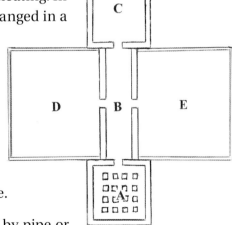

Room B seemed to be basically a corridor but with a heat vent under the floor. This measured from 6m to 9m long and 1.5m to 2.5m wide. In most sites there was a door-space in each side, which led to a larger room but these do not have a broad wall-base.

Room C was a wash room with water being led in by pipe or drain in every case. This was usually 5m by 6-9m long.

In these three rooms, the walls were about 0.8m broad and stone built, leading to the conclusion that these could be at fire risk. As these rooms with their broad walls are most commonly recognised, this is known as a linear bathhouse but this is a variation which seems to have been popular in the southern Scotland. There are two side-rooms which fit into the recesses of the other two.

On the plan, rooms D and E had narrow wall-bases, seemingly sleeper-beamed, i.e., built on a wooden base. They were away from the direct heat and thus less likely to catch fire but at the same time enjoying some of the secondary heat from B.

At Oakwood fort, the bathhouse had the same basic pattern of A being the heat chamber, B the passage and C the wash room but on a smaller scale and without the side rooms D and E.(which I may have missed.) This building was located immediately outside the fort annexe at **NT 42573 24829.** As this annexe is considered to have been a second phase addition, a space in the wall and ditch shows that the bathhouse remained in use even though it might have been a first phase construction.

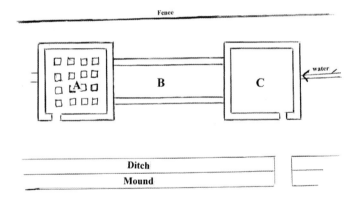

In all the cases I have found, room C is always higher than the room A because water falls while heat rises.

Having established that I was finding a fairly standard bathhouse building in or near the Roman forts in the Borders, I searched to see if there were similar constructions known in other sites. In Sir George MacDonald's report on excavations at Croy Hill in 1930-31, he notes the bathhouse '*was a long narrow building, measuring 67 feet from east to west by 12 feet from north to south. In spite of its narrowness it seemed to have been divided longitudinally and there were certainly two transverse partitions*'. That was good enough for me.

Taking a mean average of the bathhouse buildings I had found, the A, B and C rooms together formed a long narrow building measuring 70 feet by 14 feet. Not bad, but there were several things that did not quite fit.

Although the construction pattern was the same, the bathhouses beside forts and fortlets were not a standard size. The breadth was around 4m to 5m but the total length could vary from 11m to 23m. This variation could reflect the number of men that each served and the individual demands of the builders or the local availability of the material used.

THE PROBLEMS

By now I had seven bathhouses beside Roman forts, known and recently 'discovered' but had found nothing which would verify my claims and nothing could be seen – a fact that was pointed out to me by archaeologists who wanted 'proof'. I had to agree although I did point out that before Curle started to dig in the field near Newstead, nobody realised that there was a Roman baths just over the hedge either.

I have found that the main problem is proving that divining rods do actually work, for nothing unifies professional opinion more strongly than an amateur with an idea. Air photography provides photographs which can be interpreted, geophysics give a plan to be studied and guessed at, but the diviner can only record the places where the rods cross or uncross and from this, work out a plan of what might be under the ground even if nothing can be seen on the surface. Life can be hard.

The lack of finds was disappointing because I was expecting some of the brick and tile fragments which are common round the site of the known bathhouse at Trimontium but these were made in the brick and tile works beside the fort; and it is unlikely that such a heavy product would be sent to subsidiary forts.

However, it would be possible for the Roman squadies to build a functional underground furnace and passage to lead heated air through the length of the three rooms A, B and C.

The second problem was more of a common sense one. Room A with the furnace underneath, was internally 4m square or less. So this sauna room could not have held more them twelve men unless they were packed in like sweaty sardines.

The Oakwood fort was reckoned to be able to have housed around 500 men, so one small bathhouse would not be sufficient to cater for their needs of hygiene and recreation. With this in mind, I revisited the site and found that there were another two similarly shaped structures on the other side of the fence. These were at **NT 42529 24803** and **NT 42597 24831**.

Another round of the forts and provisional sites was required. Lanton fort bathhouse was at **NT 61422 21879** but there was another at **NT 61381 21961** and another at **NT 61357 21980**. They were all connected to the same drain/water supply.

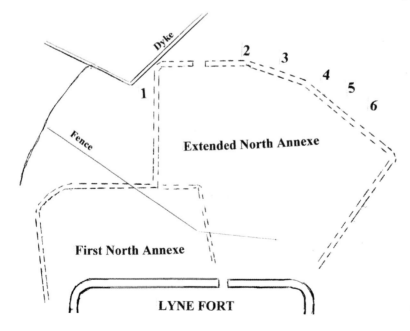

The fort at Lyne produced a similar, but more definite results with an extra five bathhouses in an arc inside the extended northern annexe of the fort. Counting the original, these were at **1. NT 18736 40743, 2. NT 18831 40782, 3. NT 18838 40729, 4. NT 18889 40709, 5. NT 18956 40481, 6. NT 18990 40651.** The same drain/pipe led water to the cisterns within the fort.

After checking on other sites that might be of Roman in origin, I decided that the criterion for Roman military construction would be the presence of a drain leading into a bathhouse. I later added 'and latrine' because both were served by the same water supply.

With so many linear bathhouses around the forts or annexes of forts, some re-thinking had to be done. They are definitely there and not the product of a fevered imagination as some may hint.

My best conclusion is that each was the domain of a century, nominally a hundred men but usually around eighty. The idea of each century of troops having its own place of recreation would appeal to the military mind which likes its troops to 'bond' with their companions, be it regiment, company or section.

Such 'Century Bathhouses' could be easily constructed in a short time from local resources. A pit dug into the ground would be the furnace to heat Room A and heat, vented through stone-built ducts or loosely packed stones, would draw it under B and C. It must be remembered that a Roman bath was not a case of soap and water but rather of extreme sweating, oil and a strigil to scrape excess oil from the body. Water was needed to close the open pores of the body before venturing outside and to wash clothing.

Rooms D and E would be the relaxation or drying rooms because even tough Roman soldiers would need somewhere to dry their clothes during a Caledonian winter.

That explanation is quite acceptable for the forts at Oakwood and Lanton Mains, each with three bathhouses. Using this as a template and provided I have not missed any others, this would infer that each was garrisoned by around two hundred and forty troops. Lyne has a story of its own which is detailed below.

> In the crises times of the First and Second World Wars, large temporary camps were thrown up to accommodate the extra troops. These tents or corrugated-iron Nissen huts were erected in company blocks housing 120 men but with no facilities. Nearby an ablutions hut was provided for washing, shaving and latrines. The Romans were likely to have a similar structure in their army.

However, there was a further complication when a different type of bathhouse began to appear in some of the larger forts. This was the more acceptable Roman bathhouse which comprised three 8m square rooms with thick walls joined end to end making a building 26m by 10m. I did find their prototypes in some Antonine Wall excavations reports so for identification I called them 'Legionary' bathhouses as they only turned up in the larger forts.

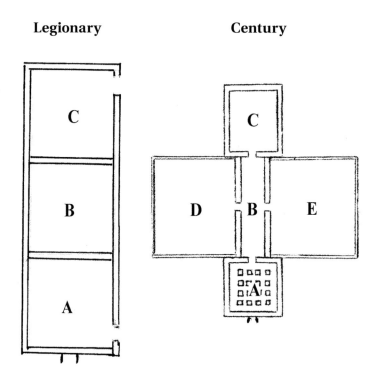

Legionary   **Century**

CHAPTER SEVEN

Major Roman Roads in the Borders

While Trimontium lay quietly undiscovered under crops of corn and grass for seventeen hundred years until James Curle began to excavate in 1909, there was one Roman construction that benefitted the Borders throughout the whole period. This was the road building programme that was planned by Roman surveyors and built by Roman pioneers.

There has been little professional study of Roman roads in the Borders other than the route of Dere Street in the Inventory of Roxburghshire. The same Inventory has a brief description of the road from Raeburnfoot to Craik and a photograph of a Roman culvert in what is now Forestry Commission ground.

Peeblesshire has a known Roman road that joins the fort at Lyne to the western branch of the roads into Scotland. A further section was noted at Edston and hypothetically traced by ground observation to Laidlawstiel on the Selkirkshire county border.

Because the Romans built roads in the Borders primarily as means of moving troops quickly to any trouble spot, there were forts, temporary camps, fortlets and watch/signal towers spread along the routes. Some are known, some are recent discoveries but still to be proved, and many others that are yet to be found. By ground appraisal along the sides of the known Roman roads, it is easy to pick out the sites likely to have been chosen for permanent or temporary settlement. As some of this is written in Selkirkshire Book One, I will be using bits of that text together with new additional information and roughly drawn illustrations because it is easier to understand drawings than the reference numbers.

Nota Bene. I am not an artist but Cath Rutherford who is, has redrawn the worst of them.

In this chapter, I will be giving most attention to the three main Roman roads which crossed the region; Dere Street which bisects the area from south to north and two east/

west roads which link Dere Street to the Annandale/Nithsdale road system through southern Scotland. These are from Craik Cross to Roxburgh and onwards to Tweedmouth and the road which leaves Trimontium, travelling up the Tweed to Lyne fort complex in Peeblesshire. I have re-travelled them with a more experienced eye.

DERE STREET

The Roman road that stretched northwards from Hadrian's Wall to the Forth was one of the two main routes into Scotland. It was much used by them and by the Anglian invaders in the 7th and 8th centuries who planted settlements along its length and named it 'Dere Street'. It continued to be one of the main roads between Scotland and England until the turnpike roads were constructed in the 18th century.

Dere Street crosses the border between Scotland and England at **NT 790 096** where a Roman fortlet is located 13m west of the road on Brownhart Law. From here, there is a line of sight across the Borders Region to the Midlothian boundary. The Inventory of Roxburghshire gives a meticulous description of route and construction methods involved in laying down Dere Street but often misses out on what lies beside the road. The report on Brownhart Law 'signal station' says 'The lack of other posts at necessary points where they should have been equally visible suggests that this one was not part of a signalling system organised along Dere Street but was intended for communication with the signal station on Ruberslaw whose summit is visible thirteen miles to the WNW'.

This is a very wrong deduction as there are a series of signal/watch towers with their attendant forts or fortlets stretching along Dere Street from Brownhart Law to Dun Law on the Mid-Lothian County boundary. What the Commissioners may have been looking for were the squashed-doughnut shapes which mark out the Gask Ridge line but in the Borders the signal/watch towers were completely made of wood. As in the Gask Ridge line, the tower was founded on a 3.5m square* with a large post in each corner and would have stood around 7m high. In the Borders, this was surrounded by a 10/12m circular enclosure of sharpened posts with a slight ditch in front. That assumption was made when I found a 0.3m slot round each tower and the illustration of an identical structure depicted in Trajan's column.

* This is the same measurement as the leather tents in marching or temporary camps.

For reasons which I will give later, I will be using the term 'watch towers' as I think their principal object was to look out for approaching enemy. Although there are a number of known signaling techniques to pass messages, it is unlikely that the signaling here was other than to light a beacon-torch as a warning to other defenders along the line.

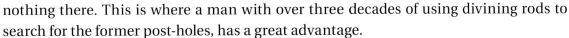

Watch Tower on Dere Street

The wooden towers left little trace on the ground to be seen or recorded and the assumption was that there was nothing there. This is where a man with over three decades of using divining rods to search for the former post-holes, has a great advantage.

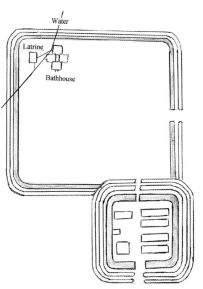

By walking along the line of Dere Street, I could find the towers and the fortlets of their attendant garrison troops. The fortlets were almost always of a uniform size and shape so it is worth giving an illustration of this to avoid future duplication. There are some variations in the size of the fortlet, the position of the annexe, its gates etc and sometimes the fort was enclosed within the annexe but in general this is the right plan.

Standard Plan of Fortlet and Annexe

A rampart and double ditch enclosed a square which varied between 18m and 22m according to the roughness of the ground and accuracy of my pacing. With this in mind, I standardised them as 20m by 20m when writing them up.

There was one gateway about 2.5m usually facing on to Dere Street and a narrow doorway which led into the adjoining annexe which was often 30m by 30m but varied in size to double that in some fortlets. Inside the annexe and as far from the main buildings as possible, were the bathhouse and latrine. These were fed from the same drain which gathered water from the slope above the complex. Some of these drains must still filter water as the bathhouse/latrine ground is often wetter than the surrounding land and this encourages moisture-seeking plants.

Externally the outer ditch is about 1m across, the inner about 1.5m and the wall/rampart base is about 1.5m. These measurements would not make for a defensible structure as both ditches would be jumpable and the wall-mound could not have been more than 1m high if built with the excavated ditch spoil alone. Looking for a more reasonable explanation, I found a slot on the outside of the rampart which would have held a post-wall. If the wall was around 2m high, the excavated spoil would have provided a raised walkway on the inside. This is feasible and a suitable explanation and why they have never been noticed before. Nineteen hundred year have rotted the wood and filled the slight trenches.

Internally, the fortlets were laid out to a standard pattern containing four barrack blocks each 12m by 4m in the major part. The minor part held one building measuring 6m or 7m by 4m and another 4m by 4m while a further shape 2m by 1m against the rampart, is likely to have been the oven. This size and shape would accommodate around 25/30 men a number sufficient to man the watch towers or fight off a small scale raiding party if necessary.

There were a few buildings inside the annexes and some beside the fortlets, usually along the line of road.

BROWNHART LAW TO WHITTON EDGE

This first section of Dere Street is through hill country which has had little arable cultivation.

1. At **NT 790 096**, the fortlet at **Brownhart Law** is the first intrusion of Dere Street into the Borders Region. Although it is claimed as a signal station, it is more likely to have been a fortlet housing troops as there are three watch tower/signal stations in a line facing north at **78446 09087.** The bathhouse and latrine are at **78560 09065** on the other side of the Border.

2. Blackhall Hill is likely to have another but I took cramp on the way from Brownhart Law which put off that inspection for another day and, preferably, another person.

(While hirpling past the Chew Green complex, I was tempted to try divining rods in the large northerly camp. There are six legionary bathhouses (3 x 8m square chambers) and a commodious latrine, 25m by 5m, inside the north wall of the biggest camp. This fits into the story of Dere Street very well. In fact, the story of the Chew Green complex would benefit from several days divining there.)

3. Woden Law. At **NT 77097 12775**, a 20m by 20m fortlet with annexe containing bathhouse and latrine was beside Dere Street. Half of it is under an old house built on the site. The watch tower is on the knowe on the other side of the road at **77034 12693**.

4. Kale Water Crossing. At **NT 75930 13626**, Dere Street crossed the Kale Water by means of a raised wooden platform about 40m long. The supporting posts were in pairs 3.5m apart and in two rows. This is the usual way for Roman roads to cross burns and generally wet places. The road line appears as a bridge mound in the grounds of Towford Outdoor Centre.

5. Pennymuir Camps. At **NT 755 140**, the four camps at Pennymuir are claimed to be the best preserved temporary camps in Scotland. Camps A and B were mapped by General Roy to appear in his *Military Antiquities, 1793*. Camps C and D were discovered from air photographs in the 1940s. I am not convinced that the description 'temporary camp' can be applied to A or B as both were built on a massive scale and must have been used many times.

Camp A

Camp A is 520m by 320m with a rampart base 4.5m and still standing 1.2m high. The single ditch is around 5m wide and over 1m deep. Five gates are visible, varying from 17m to 20m wide. Using divining rods I could determine that the gateways had seven facing posts on the outside and six on the inside. This is evidence of a substantial towered gate and is much more than is required for a temporary camp. A camp of this size is reckoned to be capable of housing two legions for a short time.

Camp B

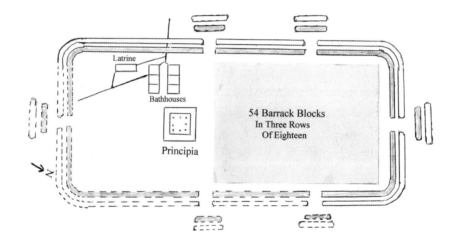

Camp B is about a fifth of the size of A, measuring 292m by 125m. It had utilised part of the east and south ramparts of Camp A but this area has been ploughed out by modern agriculture.

Four gates remain and these measure a uniform 17m. They have the same-seven post frontage with six posts behind. These cannot be other than fortified towers. Inside the perimeter, the northern two-thirds are taken up by three rows of barrack blocks, each 40m by 4.5m, comparable to the barrack blocks at Trimontium and Bonjedward. This part of the camp is in very rough pasture with tufted grass mixed with wet holes where cattle have been champing. Nothing can be seen from air or ground.

On the other third, there is a hollow square building with outer sides about 25m long, the buildings inside 5m wide and a row of postholes round the inner walls. This is the size and shape of a Principia; and it probably is.

A concentration of molehills led me to two bathhouses of the 'legionary' type and a latrine 12m by 4m, suggesting that this camp/fort was expected to house a large number of men, even if it was only for a short time. Its size shape and layout suggests that this was a regular fort but the location makes that doubtful as it would be too difficult to supply although there is no reason why there should not have been a small garrison here for maintenance.

My suggestions is that both A and B should be looked on as 'transit' camps available to passing troops who would be spared the work involved in building a new temporary camp each night. This idea became more feasible as I progressed along Dere Street.

It has been suggested that the larger Pennymuir camps were the semi-permanent billets of troops practising field manoeuvers investing the native fort at Woden Law as well as housing passing units. This is quite feasible.

Camp C is a normal temporary camp with slight defences and a ditch 1m wide and 0.5m deep. This was seen where modern draining cut through the defences. Divining rods showed rows of tents in the normal pattern.

Camp D appears to be Roman but may not be as there was a 17th century inn on this site when Dere Street was one of the main roads into and out of Scotland. If it is Roman the chances are that D was a waggon park beside the road but that is a guess!

6. Pennymuir Fortlet. At **NT 75479 14261** and just north of Camp A, a 20m by 20m fortlet appears on air photographs. It has an annexe complete with small bathhouse and latrine. There is a watch tower in the thick wood to the north of the fortlet.

This fortlet is in the pattern of those to be found along the defence line of Dere Street but it is possible that it may have billeted a small number of troops who maintained the above camps when they were not in use.

7. Pennymuir Temporary Camp E. At **NT 75449 14795** to the north of Camp C, there is another temporary camp measuring 120m by 90m. It has a rampart and single ditch with the tent postholes and rubbish pits of a normal marching camp. Unusually, there are two bathhouses of the legionary type and a latrine 12m by 4m in an annexe tacked on outside of the north-east corner of the camp. Obviously this was a maintained transit camp.

This was an unusual find in my tramp along Dere Street and I debated starting from the beginning again to look for bathhouses and latrines in the marching camps along the route. There is no reason why camps that were in intermittent use should not have these facilities on a maintained basis.

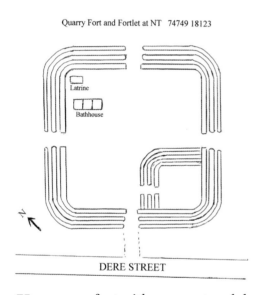

Quarry Fort and Fortlet at NT 74749 18123

Latrine

Bathhouse

DERE STREET

8. Trestle Cairn. At **NT 75360 16010,** there is a 20m by 20m fortlet with annexe containing bathhouse and latrine to east. Watch tower is at **75193 16090.**

9. Upper Chatto. At **NT 75283 17286**, there is a 20m by 20m fortlet with annexe to south-east containing bathhouse and latrine.

At **NT 74876 17965**, there is a watch tower with the usual four posts in a 3.5m square. This appears in the Inventory of Roxburghshire, No 342, as a 'cairn'.

10. Quarry fort/fortlet at **NT 74749 18123**. Below the watch tower is an old quarry where there is a 75m square fort with rampart and double ditches. Inside this is a 'legionary' bathhouse and latrine in the north-east corner of the enclosure. In the south-west corner of the fort, a 20m by 20m fortlet uses the corner of the fort for two of its sides. Traces of fort and fortlet can be seen on the ground.

It is likely that the large fort was originally occupied when the quarry was being used to provide stonework and rubble for the construction of Dere Street.

WHITTON EDGE TO JEDFOOT

Other than a slight turn in the road at Whitton Edge, Dere Street lies in a straight line to Jedfoot where there is a complex of forts and camps.

11. Townfoot Hill. At **NT 73455 18781**, there is a 20m by 20m fortlet with annexe containing small bathhouse and latrine. Watch tower at **73439 18653**.

12. Shothead. At **NT 71647 19845**, there is a 20m by 20m fortlet with annexe containing small bathhouse and latrine. Watch tower at **NT 71555 19326**.

The watch tower at **NT 702 205** probably fits in with Cappuck fortlet below.

13. Cappuck Fortlet. Air photography has revealed a number of marching camps along Dere Street on either side of the Cappuck fort. While studying some of the RCAHMS photos, I noticed some unusual marks in a field at **NT 69935 20972**, about 400m south of the fort. Inside the faint lines of a marching camp, there was a 20m by 20m fortlet with

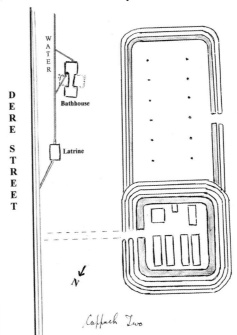

small bathhouse and latrine. An interesting annexe measuring 40m by 28m, lay on the south side; interesting because I could find only one gate which opened on the side away from Dere Street. There were no buildings in the annexe but two rows of posts 10m apart. There may be a further enclosure containing the bathhouse and latrine, which I have missed.

This could be one of the normal watch-keeping garrisons but another suggestion is that this was designed for a cavalry unit as a cavalry turma of thirty-two men would fit into this size of fortlet. Likewise, the posts could be for two rows of horse lines with the gate placed to lead to the open country for grazing.

14. Cappuck Fort. The next known fort along Dere Street on the way north is Cappuck which lies on the east bank of Oxnam Water. It has been presumed that it was placed here to guard the bridge but this is unlikely because the Oxnam Water is quite wadeable. Criticism that the site had no 'good outlook for watching or signalling' was solved by the watch tower noted above.

The fort itself was excavated in 1886, 1911-12 and 1949 and a time scale of occupation worked out. It was reckoned to have been garrisoned during all phases of the Roman occupation of southern Scotland. Air photographs taken in 1976 added timber palisades to the defences of the fort. But no attention was paid to the ground in the immediate vicinity and it is seldom that a Roman fort existed without an annexe or settlement of some description growing beside or near it.

So it had to be looked for and the first step was to find the drain or pipe which took water into the fort or annexe. At **NT 69533 21070**, the drain was found. It led to two bathhouses of the usual century pattern and a latrine measuring 8m by 5m. As these were well away from the excavated fort site, further searching led to an annexe on the south side of the fort, the only feasible area for expansion. Divining this shows that an area of 150m by 170m has been enclosed by a rampart and two ditches and that two lines of small buildings were on a road leading into the fort.

At **NT 69509 21194** there was a gateway into the fort, or rather into one of the forts that had stood on the same site. This gateway does not show up on APs as it was probably from the second or third construction of the fort and would be built over in the final phase. The point that does stand out is that it is unusual to find a thick rampart and double ditch round an annexe.

On the west side of the annexe, the ground drops steeply to the Oxnam Water. A raised mound about 4m wide runs along the top of the bank and represents the rampart on the west side of the annexe. This can be seen on the ground and as a broad white band in a Royal Commission AP of 1976.

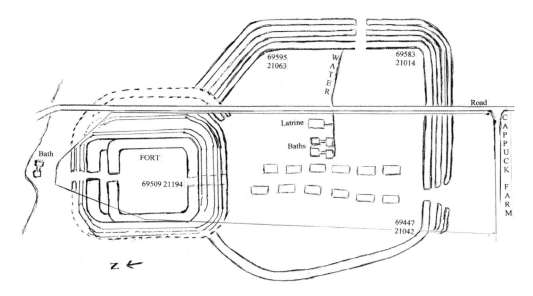

It was an added bonus to find a small bathhouse at **NT 69557 21300** on a flat beside the burn. This is probably the bathhouse of the first small fort on site.

15. Ulston Moor One. At **NT 68835 21793**, a 20m by 20m fortlet with an annexe containing a bathhouse and latrine. Watch tower was to west.

16. Ulston Moor Two. At **NT 68319 22276**, a 20m by 20m fortlet with an annexe containing a bathhouse and latrine, Watch tower at **68265 22200**.

17. Mount Ulston One. At **NT 67524 22885**, a 20m by 20m fortlet with an annexe containing a bathhouse and latrine. Watch tower at **67440 22801**.

18. Mount Ulston Two. At **NT 67209 23070**, a 20m by 20m fortlet with an annexe containing a bathhouse and latrine. Watch tower at **67218 22945**.

19. Mount Hooly. At **NT 66639 23587**, there is the 20m by 20m fortlet which I had dug by JCB some years previously but didn't recognise its largely wooden construction. The 30m x 30m annexe is on the east side with bathhouse and latrine at **66650 23601**. The watchtower is at **66621 23377**.

20. Jedfoot. Where Dere Street crosses the Jed and Teviot rivers at Jedfoot, logic demands that there must have been a Roman fort as well as a large number of temporary camps in the area as this was a natural over-night stopping place for troops moving along the main road north. The bridge across the Teviot is at **NT 65631 24368,** exactly where the road is shown to cross the river on the 19th century maps.

By ground observation, the most obvious place for a permanent Roman fort is at Jerdonfield **NT 650 230** or at Bonjedward **NT 655 235.** The area was progressively photographed by Professor St Joseph who decided that the knowe on which Jerdonfield sits, must have been the site of the fort that guarded the crossings of both rivers. His excavations here produced no positive results. In 1992, I tried the same and found nothing either.

Professor St Joseph flew many air surveys over the haughs between the rivers and on the south side of the Jed, looking for the marching camps which he was convinced must be there but with no success. Everybody knew that temporary camps had to be there but, as far as I know, none have shown up on air photographs despite many attempts.

The explanation for this is simple and logical - this is a sandy soil. The Romans dug their single ditch, banking the spoil as a rampart for their temporary camps. Even although they may have filled in the ditch the next day, the profile of the ditch in sandy soil never retained subsequent rainfall and thus couldn't produce the extra growth in the young crop which is required to show as a deeper band on air photographs. Similarly, rain simply soaked into the vestiges of the sandy banks and did not produce lighter lines in the crop.

The result of this is that young crops on sandy soil grow at a uniform rate, thereby making life difficult for air photographers. Of course the same soil conditions apply to geophysics which also relies on magnetic/electrical responses to give variations in readings. Both sciences respond best to a clay soil ditch which holds water and a bank that sheds it for the best results.

However sandy soil does not seem to inhibit the use of divining rods which produce excellent results even although many believe this could not possibly be correct. It is ironic that most Roman temporary camps would be sited beside a river where clean water was available but where the soil is sandy and least responsive to air photographs or geophysics.

Scotland claims to have the greatest proportion of Roman temporary/marching camps. How many more yet to be discovered?

I found traces of many in the haughs of Mount Hooly and Jerdonfield but only noted a few. There was one camp at Mount Hooly that I thought a bit odd when I first found it some twenty years ago. It is sited at Mount Hooly on the south side of the joined rivers. It has a rampart and single ditch, measures about 220m by 170m with its corners at **66774 24047, 66882 23860, 67013 24022** and **66923 24167**. Three gates on the long sides are at 60 pace intervals; two gates on shorter sides had the same spacing*. Inside of the camp, there are rows of rubbish pits and tents set in the standard pattern.

There are at least three camps of that size in the square kilometre of flat haughland in front of Jerdonfield. To the east of Mount Hooly, there is a very large camp that may fit into the pattern of 165-acre Severan temporary camps are known from Trimontium northwards but I have not yet managed to find the time (or the stamina) to mark out its perimeters. Must do better – will look for bathhouses and latrines next time.

*This sixty pace measurement was to prove enlightening in the future.

20. Bonjedward Fort Complex.

With no luck at Jerdonfield, the other possible site for a permanent fort was at Bonjedward where a ridge runs down through the flat lands to the junction of the Jed and Teviot. In fact I found two forts as well as a fortlet further up the ridge. This was quite expected as it was the logical place for a fort and the Romans were very logical in siting their forts.

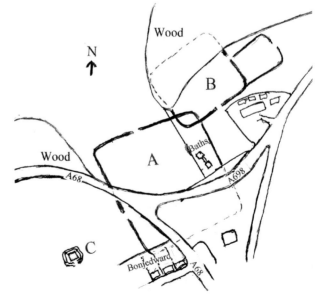

Fort A at **NT 65662 23690**, is the largest and probably the first to be built. Nearly square with sides about 180m long, it has a rampart base 6m thick and two ditches, the inner 6m wide and the outer 5m. Part of the east rampart is still over 1m high with the two divined ditches being filled in when it collapsed. The gates on the north and west had seven postholes on the outer edge and six inside. These were the same at those at Trimontium and Pennymuir.

Fort B at **NT 65689 23685**, is less massively built with rampart and two ditches. It is c 90m by 60m? but this is difficult to be sure of as half of it lies within a wood. Several barrack buildings 28m by 4.5m were stepped out and the south and east gates were noted. An annexe c 90m by 50m on the east side contained two rows of houses and a number of pits.

The east side of A and the south half of B are in a field which has never been cultivated. This has left an impressive east rampart of A and a raised platform which is the south side of B. A bathhouse of standard Borders pattern was either within A or from a south annexe of B.

Fortlet C stands on a flat platform at **NT 65442 23503**. It has a standard size 20m square internally, is double ditched with a gateway facing south and stands within a 60m square enclosure. The small bathhouse and latrine are at **NT 65454 23477**. Slightly uphill from the fortlet, a signal tower at **NT 65422 23411** has a clear view of the watch tower on Eildon Hill North and the Fairnington one below. Trees blind the view southwards.

21. Jerdonfield Haugh. With over 3 square kilometres of the haughs around Jerdonfield and Mount Hooly known to have been covered by temporary camps at least once and probably many times, I have long thought that there had to have been a supply depot in this area.

If a Roman force left Corbridge to march north, they were facing nearly sixty miles of rough country through the Cheviots before arriving at Jedfoot. This would have been a three or four days march and their supplies would be depleted by the time they got there. To get bulk supplies delivered to that point, it seemed logical that the Roman commissariat would use river transport, the codicarae which were small punt-like boats capable of carrying ten tons each trip. It is an eight-mile trip from the junction of the Teviot and Tweed to the junction of the Jed and Teviot. So it seemed a good idea for me to walk the river banks to see if the divining rods could pick up a quay or some signs of an enclosure.

There was one at **NT 65869 24264,** near the junction of the Jed and Teviot. It was about 80m by 60m, quite strongly walled and ditched with twelve buildings in two rows of six. They were a uniform size 20m by 5m with wide walls and two buttresses on each side of the buildings. They could hardly be anything other than grain stores.

 Directly to the south of the granaries at **NT 65891 24197**, there is depression which marks the line of the former Jerdonfield Burn. This line has been preserved by a number of oak tree stumps. Following the curve of the former burn, I found five legionary bathhouses (3 x 8m square chambers) and five latrines 20m by 4m, following the same curve. All were fed by a drain/pipe which came from the higher reaches of the burn. It is more than likely that the course of the burn has been directed along the foot of the bank by Roman hands.

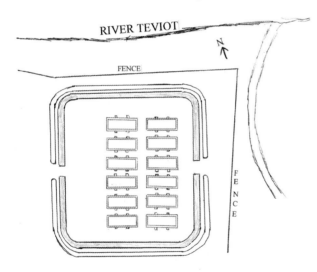

Granaries at Jed Water/ Teviot Junction

These would be intended to serve the complex of temporary camps which are numerous on the river haughs at Jerdonfield and Mount Hooly.

Jedfoot to Trimontium on Tweed at Leaderfoot.
After crossing the Teviot, Dere Street is clearly visible through the Monteviot grounds and up to the ridge of The Baron's Folly. It runs in the same straight line to St Boswells, curves round Newtown and then down to the Tweed at Leaderfoot.

22. Howden Woods. At **NT 64054 25696,** there is a 20m by 20m fortlet with annexe containing bathhouse and latrine. Watch tower is on a ridge to the west at **63768 25392**.

23. Fairnington. At **NT 63251 26337,** there is a 20m by 20m fortlet on a ridge on Fairnington land which commands a wide view of the western Borders as far the hill of upper Roxburghshire and Selkirkshire.

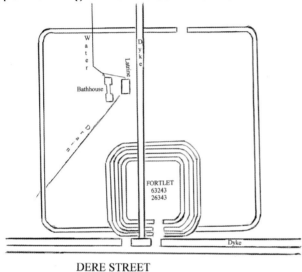

DERE STREET

The fortlet stands within an annexe enclosure 60m square with latrine and bathhouse in the north-east corner. Watch tower is at **63362 26407.**

24. Lilliard's Edge. At **NT 62101 27442,** there is a fortlet 40m by 20m with four gateways and a 70m by 60m annexe containing bathhouse and latrine. The watch tower is at **61823 27382.**

25. Forest Lodge. At **NT 60636 28832** there is a 20m by 20m fortlet with 30m by 30m annexe on the east containing bathhouse and latrine. Watch tower is at **60600 28679.**

26. St Boswell/Selkirk Road. At **NT 58670 30703** there is a 20m by 20m watch tower with annexe to the south containing bathhouse and latrine. Watch tower is at **58609 30766.** This tower is beside the mobile telephone mast.

27. Whitelee. At **NT 57423 30772**, there is a 20m by 20m fortlet with annexe to the south.

This does not contain the bathhouse/latrine which are in a separate enclosure further down the slope at **57507 30308**. Watch tower is at **57295 31012**.

28. Newtown. At **NT 57059 31622**, there is a 20m by 20m fortlet with annexe to the south containing bathhouse and latrine. Watch tower is at **56914 31718**.

Both Whitelee and Newtown fortlets are to the west of the line of Dere Street. This is likely to be deliberate as the area between the fortlet line and Dere Street has produced Roman coins and Samian pottery.

29. Eildon. At **NT 56977 32740** there is a 60m by 40m fortlet within what seems to be a native settlement. Watch tower at **56916 32770**. This has reverted to the line of Dere Street. The bathhouse and latrine are in a 60m by 60m annexe to the east of the fortlet.

30. Rhymer's Stone. At **NT 56826 33557**, there is a 20m by 20m fortlet with an annexe to the east containing bathhouse and latrine. Watchtower is at **56681 33477**.

Around the fort of Trimontium and its annexes, there are a number of known temporary camps and many more fragmentary walls and ditches which do not fit into the photographic record. So it was no great surprise that I found that the lower part of the Boglie Burn had been claimed to supply water to six legionary bathhouses and six latrines 20m by 4m in the annexe of a camp to the south of the main fort. The water is taken from the burn **at NT 57453 33556** and supplied the facilities from **5741 33617** to **57568 33739**. This double line of bathhouses and latrines follows the curve of the lower burn and is remarkably like that of Jerdonfield and at St Leonards which I had previously noted.

This discovery prompted me to look again at the Annay haughs laying to the west of the Trimontium Fort complex. This is a large flat area beside the river Tweed which has more than the one temporary camp identified from air photographs. The site would have been ideal for troops in transit being flat, easily dug, and with a convenient water supply – but a sandy soil does not respond very well to air photography.

Millmount, Newstead. There was one large camp whose corners were at **(1) NT 55079 34344, (2) NT 55997 34660, (3) NT 55491 34302 and (4) NT 55531 34701**. Although the

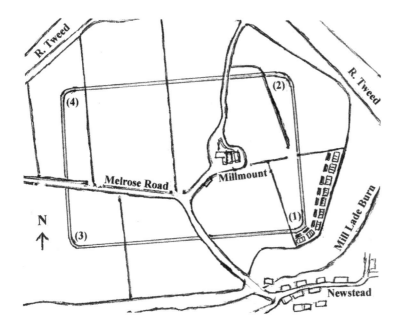

gates and tituli are not shown on the illustration, the camp passed the tentpole-hole tests with flying colours – this had been a tented camp. My interest was to see how the camp was positioned with the line of the Mill Lade, a natural burn that ran along the bottom of the bank to the south of the haugh. In between the rampart/ditch of the camp and the Mill Lade burn, there were nine legionary bathhouses and corresponding latrines 16m by 4m curving round the slightly raised bank known as Alice Knowe. With a line of bathhouses/latrines in position in either side of the fort complex, Trimontium must have been as much a focal transit location as a garrison fort.

31. Ravenswood. At **NT 57489 34422**, there is a 20m by 20m fortlet with bathhouse and latrine in annexe to north-east. Watchtower is at **57374 34295** just outside the East Annexe of the Trimontium Fort.

N.B. The line of fortlets from the south leads to the site of the Roman Bridge at Leaderfoot and the line of fortlets northwards starts on the opposite side of the river. So there is little question that the bridge was in use when the fortlets were built.

LEADERFOOT TO LAUDER

So far there has been an indiscriminate mixture of forts, fortlets and transit/temporary camps along the line of Dere Street. After crossing the Tweed, there is a parting of the ways with air photographs showing a number of temporary camps on the lower land beside the Leader Water while the constructed Dere Street with its string of fortlets, kept on the higher ground to the west.

THE CAMPS

As air photography showed convincing details of temporary camps at Drygrange, Blainslie and Kedslie, there was the assumption that Dere Street ran along the bottom of the valley. So I sallied forth to investigate with divining rods to prove or disprove this theory.

Drygrange. When a linear mark across the Camp Hill near Drygrange was identified as a Roman temporary or marching camp, I was very doubtful for the simple reason that the ground was too steep to pitch tents with any hope of comfort and I had already identified that same line was the part of Dere Street which left the East/West road about seventy metres west of Leaderfoot Farm before heading northwards.

As a scientist, the late Bill Lonie probably had as much belief in fairies as he did in divining rods but he was a good reader of ground. He published a paper on Dere Street north of the Tweed and made the same conclusion as I had, conceding that divining rods may have some use after all.

The idea of a road and a temporary camp together is not mutually exclusive but when I went back with divining rods to look for tent-pole holes to prove the site, I couldn't find any. So I think that this identification is a misjudgement but will wait for excavation to decide.

Kedslie. temporary camp encloses 19 acres and passes all the tent-pole tests. There is an annexe attached to the south half of the east rampart at **NT 55844 39827**. This holds 2 legionary bathhouses and a latrine measuring 12m by 4m.

Blainslie. temporary camp encloses 45 acres and passes the tent-pole tent. Air photographs show an annexe 70m by 65m on the south. This holds 2 legionary bathhouses and a latrine 14m by 4m.

Conclusions. The Kedslie and Blainslie camps and probably part of the much larger camp at St Leonards are likely to have been spaced construction camps for the troops working on Dere Street. The mod/cons suggest a use of several months.

REVERTING TO THE LINE OF DERE STREET

32. Drygrange Mains. At **NT 57286 35585**, there is a 20m by 20m fortlet with annexe containing bathhouse and latrine to the east. Watch tower at **57283 35578**.

33. Kittyfield. At **NT 56631 35770**, there is a 20m by 20m fortlet with annexe to east containing bathhouse and latrine. Watchtower is c 300m away at **56368 35891**.

34. Craigsford Mains. At **NT 55567 337269,** there is a 20m by 20m fortlet within a 60m by 60m annexe which contains bathhouse and latrine. Watch tower is at **55472 37240**.

35. Sorrowlessfield Mains. At **NT 55903 36669**, there is a 20m by 20m fortlet with annexe to south containing bathhouse and latrine. Watch tower within wood at **55826 36680**.

36. Easter Housebyres. At **NT 54727 37885** there is a fortlet 40m by 20m with four gateways and an annexe 70m x 65m. The baths and latrine are within the lower ground of the enclosure at **NT 54678 37827**. A watch tower lay in a wood just east of the fortlet and a palisaded enclosure had been added on the north side.

37. Cairneymount. At **NT 53907 39541** there is a 20m by 20m fortlet with a 30m by 30m annexe containing bathhouse and latrine on the north. The four posts of a watch tower are within a scooped enclosure at **NT 54004 39567**. This enclosure has a 6m wide bank around it and several stone-built houses? This needs further investigation.

38. Kedslie Hill. At **NT 53621 40746**, there is a 20m by 20m fortlet with a 30m by 30m annexe containing bathhouse and latrine on the west. The watch tower is at **53489 40645**.

39. Jeaniefield. At **NT 53162 42554**, a 20m by 20m fortlet lay immediately beside Dere Street within an enclosure 70m by 70m which had the bathhouse and latrine in the south-west corner. There were two signal towers 15m apart on a ridge at **NT 53170 42710**. This is unusual and may represent two different phases or it could be two contemporary towers to be used together to indicate urgent help required. Also, I may have missed one.

40. Middle Blainslie. At **NT 53932 44336**, there is a 20m by 20m fortlet with annexe containing bathhouse and latrine to the south-east. Watch tower is at **53816 44805**.

41. St Leonards. The marching camp at St Leonards was identified by St Joseph in 1948 and subsequently. Enclosing 173 acres, it is claimed as the largest camp so far recorded and is thought to be one of four used by Severan forces in the re-invasion of AD 209.

Remembering the concentration of legionary bathhouses at Chew Green, Pennymuir (2 & 5), Jerdonfield, Trimontium and eventually Oxton, I tried divining rods on the outside of the north-west side of the camp which runs parallel with the Milsieburn, leaving a space of about 30m between. This space holds seven legionary bathhouses and seven latrines 20m by 4m which cover the area between **54474 45881** and **54351 45745**.

It may have been that the camp was only a one-night occupation during the Severan campaign if that reading is correct, but it was also part of the line of permanently maintained transit camps along the line of Dere Street as well.

There is a fort 60m by 40m with rampart and two ditches at **NT 54810 45625** on the top of the hill. An annexe 60m by 40m lies on the west side. This site needs a lot more investigation to reveal its secrets.

42. Woodheads. At **NT 54058 46172**, there is a 20m by 20m fortlet with annexe containing bathhouse and latrine to the west. Watch tower is at **53906 46106**.

43. Lauder. At **NT 51872 48947** there was a 20m by 20m fortlet with a 60m by 50m annexe containing a small bathhouse and latrine. Across Dere Street (and the old Light Railway track) the signal tower was at **51774 48886**.

LAUDER TO DUN LAW

This is flat ground until Oxton before Dere Street starts climbing over the Fala Hills.

44. Blackchester. At **NT 510 508,** there is a 20m by 20m fortlet with annexe containing bathhouse and latrine. Watch tower is at **508 507**. This is in the middle of a temporary camp.

45. Nether Howden. Following Dere Street, a fort was found at **NT 50559 53007**. This measured 90m by 60m, was double-ditched with gateways in each side. A 60m by 60m annexe containing two century bathhouses and a latrine lay on the east while a larger annexe which had been extended several times, lay on the west. This larger annexe contained two rows of houses fronting on to a section of Dere Street which was very visible across the field leading to the village of Oxton. The watch tower was at **50441 53019**.

46. Oxton Fort. Passing through Oxton, Dere Street went on to the Oxton and Channelkirk Forts**.** From Selkirkshire Book One. '*When the Roman fort at Oxton was discovered by air photography in the 1960s, I knew the site was overlooked on two sides by higher ground and was a most unlikely place for a defensive Roman fort. Yet it was very obviously of Roman construction, a small fort with a large annexe and assumed to be of Flavian construction although only Antonine pottery had been found on the site.*

In fact, the air photographs showed a small fort with a large annexe and several small ones. This was an interesting small fort with possibilities, none of them obvious.

In 2012, I took divining rods into the fort to see what the large annexe held. It had been speculated that it was to allow travellers to rest overnight before tackling the Soutra hills and that there is likely to be a corresponding fort on Soutra Mains Farm beside the Dean Burn.

What I found was ten rows of barrack blocks 20m by 4.5m and there were sixteen in the row, making a total of one hundred and sixty within the annexe. At the lower, south end of the annexe, there was a legionary bathhouse of three 8m square chambers (and probably several more that I had missed) and a latrine 18m by 5m. On the north side of the fort, there was another annexe 60m square which contained a standard century bathhouse and latrine.

This site was very similar to the transit camp at Pennymuir B. My interpretation is that Oxton was a small fort with a permanent garrison and its own annexe and was placed there to maintain the 160 barrack blocks for itinerant marching troops.

47. Channelkirk Fort. Some years ago, I was looking at old maps and found the words 'ROMAN CAMP (Site of)' beside the Manse and graveyard of Channelkirk church. This had been noted but dismissed by several archaeologists but I felt it was worth investigating with divining rods.

These indicated a nearly square double-ditched fort with gateways in the middle of each side and, unlike the Oxton fort, was on a good defensive position. The wall base was approximately 3.5m, the inner ditch 4.5m and the outer ditch 4m. There were roads into the fort and rectangular buildings inside. This was the Roman fort that had been originally noted by the early mapmakers. In 2010, I took GPS readings at the internal corners for future reference. They were at **NT 48117, 54589, NT 48022 54459** and **NT 48120 54402.**

Since then, I believe that this fort has been confirmed by air photography. There is a standard bathhouse and latrine at **47891 54414.**

While looking round the site for further traces of Roman activity, I found a temporary camp beside the Oxton fort and a native settlement close by. These have been also proven by air photography.

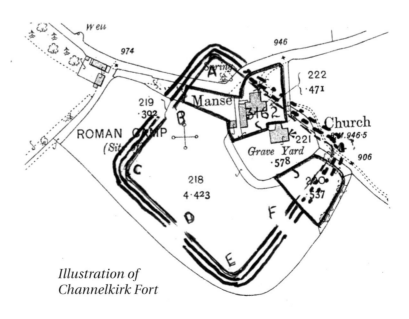

Illustration of Channelkirk Fort

85

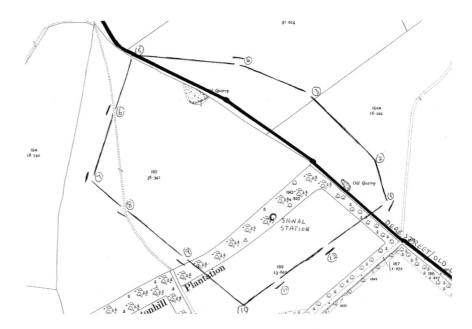

48. Channelkirk Marching Camp. Leaving the Channelkirk Fort, the road is quite visible as a broad mound passing through the known 165 acre Severan marching camp at **NT 475 548**. Though this camp is the right size, and shaped rather like the one at St Leonard's, it is not well situated, being on an exposed hill and with no bulk water supply. In the strip of wood that bisects the camp, there is a signal station at **NT 47619 56720** which is in a 9m square stone-walled enclosure.

I took the precaution of GPS-ing the gates and corners.

Number	Height	Latitude(NT)	Longitude(BNG)	
1.	1067ft	47845	54757	Gate
2.	1055ft	47849	54838	Corner
3.	1989ft	47723	54970	Gate
4.	1085ft	47606	55034	Gate
5.	1097ft	47373	55022	Gate/Corner
6.	1118ft	47318	54947	Gate
7.	1114ft	47243	54826	Gate/Corner

8.	1152ft	47338	54759	Gate
9.	1147ft	47462	54651	Gate
10.	1107ft	47534	54540	Corner
11.	1097ft	47612	54576	Gate
12.	1073ft	47713	54627	Gate

The wall base of this camp is approximately 2m across and the ditch is 3/3.5m wide. All the gates have a protecting titulus. Although Dere Street passes through gate 5, gate 1 is offset from the road.

49. Glengelt. At **NT 47285 55200**, there is a 20m by 20m fortlet with annexe containing standard bathhouse and a 10m by 4m latrine. Watch tower is at **47079 55510**. This tower has been filled with soil, probably to stabilise it against the wind.

50. Wind Farm. At **NT 46564 56531**, there is a 20m by 20m fortlet with annexe containing bathhouse and latrine. Watch tower is at **46294 56525**.

51. Dun Law. The last fortlet and watch tower along the Borders Region section of Dere Street is at **NT 45619 57390**. It is one of the 20m by 20m fortlets with an annexe measuring 65m by 50m which contains two century bathhouses and a latrine at **NT 45579 57354**. About 200m uphill on the top of the Dun Law, signal towers once stood at **NT 46010 57536**. I use 'signal' and plural because there is a row of three towers of the normal wooden construction with another in front. The row of three with 9m spaces between must represent the need to send a special message.

From Dun Law you can see Fife, the Lothians, the Cheviots, the Hills of the Leithen Water and Peeblesshire, most of the Berwickshire coast and the Borders Region. So three blazing beacons on Dun Law would send that message over a wide area.

CONCLUSIONS

The sites are there and though my conclusions may be wrong, I will give them anyway. After mapping out the sites, I realised that they fell into two distinct groupings.

The forts and maintained transit camps of Chew Green, Pennymuir 1, 2 and 5, Cappuck,

Bonjedward, Trimontium, St Leonards and Oxton represent Dere Street as a road for moving sizable numbers of troops. With the forts/camps spaced along the route, there was no need to prepare a defensive laager every time the marchers stopped for the night, especially when the maintained transit camps came with all mod cons in situ. This made sense. These would in use when the territory marched through was in friendly hands.

The situation changed when examining the line of 38 fortlets with the standard size of 20m by 20m which included the provision of bathhouses and latrines. These cannot be other than of Roman military construction and use and there may be more that I have missed. But the question is why were they built and when.

My theory is that during this fortlet period, Dere Street was a fortified road frontier as is known in other parts of the Roman Empire. Running from south to north, it does not represent any presently-known frontier between a Roman province and a hostile native population. However, there has always been the theory that the Votadini in Berwickshire and the East Coast were friendly towards the Romans whereas the Selgovae in the mid-Borders were violently opposed. I had gradually come to that conclusion from the clues I had been collecting along Dere Street but later had found that this is not a new idea. W.S. Hanson in his book *Agricola and the Conquest of the North 1987* suggests *'It is difficult to avoid the conclusion that the Venicones, like the Votadini, had Roman sympathies and may even have had their territory protected by treaty'.* Hopefully, my finds along Dere Street will go some way to proving that theory.

If this reasoning is correct, it is more than probable that there would be a spaced garrison placed along the border line to guard what was, in effect, a Roman protectorate. The fragmented land of the western Borders makes it unlikely that tribal units could form a large enough force to repel the Roman invaders, so opposition would take the form of hit and run raids to secure plunder and discomfit the enemy. The best way to counter this would be a series of closely-linked fortlets with quick methods of communication placed along the road line to give early warning of raiders and time for the small garrisons to join up to repel them.

It is worth noting that a very similar aggressive/defensive situation was still in operation in the late 16th century Borders, the time of the reivers. The thieves, rogues and robbers known by the generic term of 'reivers', inhabited the marginal lands at the tops of the Border valleys and to survive the harsh conditions, had to raid into the better, lower-lying lands to the east for sustenance and booty. Small bands of reivers carrying out raids could be repulsed by local strongmen but when larger bodies invaded, warnings of their approach were given by lighting balefires on prominent hills.

If Dere Street had continued in a similar fashion across the Lothians as far as Camelon, it could have joined up with the Gask Ridge road line of signal/watch towers to make one long boundary? If it did, the Romans would have had a protectorate along the east coast of Scotland which included the Votadini and Venicones.

A few questions for consideration. Although the fortlets were of a very uniform ground plan and have to be of military construction, who manned them? Were they detachments from full-time auxiliary army units or part-time volunteers receiving wages in kind from the local community? Or a mixture of both?

As to dating, the fortified road suggestion could apply to two periods. As noted above, the fortlet line crosses the Tweed at Leaderfoot, the site of the second bridge – the first was on the west side of the Trimontium fort. Since it avoids contact with the fort, it is reasonable to deduce that there was no garrison there when the defence line was in place and the same reasoning would apply to the fortlet beside Pennymuir camps. So we have to look for the periods when these conditions would fit.

The most likely is the twenty-five year period AD 105 – 140. when the legions are reckoned to have scuttled back to the Stanegate line, afterwards Hadrian's Wall, but it is feasible that they left a defensive line along Dere Street to protect friendly tribes with a view to returning to re-claim the territory. Such troops would be easily supplied via the East Coast seaboard.

The same conditions were in place after AD 184 when the permanent Roman garrison at Trimontium was again withdrawn to the line of Hadrian's Wall. We don't know what happened to the fabric of Dere Street for the next twenty-five years but it was evidently in good enough repair in AD 209 for the Imperial army to march through the Borders to assemble at Trimontium before proceeding up Lauderdale and into the Lothians. If this was the period when the fortlet line was manned, the garrisons could also have been road repairers.

There may even be a series of fortlets behind or near the watch-towers of the Gask Ridge for, despite long and meticulous excavation, there little or no evidence that the towers were permanently inhabited?

More importantly, could the above be proved to the satisfaction of all? Yes it could, provided someone was prepared to excavate two trenches across to walls and ditches of 38 fortlets to confirm the post-palisade, and a magnetometer was ran over the hot end of a large number of bathhouses, or even some of them. This challenge I will leave to others.

CRAIK TO ROXBURGH

In the middle 1990s, I spent part of two summers tracing Roman roads through the Borders, mainly that which was called 'the kingis grete rode from Annan to Rocesburgh' in the time of Robert the Bruce.

This was done by logical deduction, ground searching and, of course, divining rods. I started with an advantage in that I had worked on many of the places where traces of the road remain but in most there are no visible surface indications and you have to depend on the divining rods to keep you on track, literally. Where the putative road approached a burn, there was a bridge-mound on either side with a series of post holes in pairs between. These were about 3.5 metres apart. Obviously this was a bridge, or rather a raised walkway, to get the troops across without getting their feet wet. When I found this evidence of human construction, I knew that I was on the right path.

Of this reconstructed bridge, only the post-holes would give evidence of its being and they were easily found with divining rods.

Craik – Roman Fort and Temporary Camps. The Roman road across Craik Moor was identified by Dr Ian Richmond in 1945 and further evidence of Roman road-making was uncovered when a stone-built, road-culvert was exposed at **NT 342 077.**

Although the Roman road has suffered considerably by the forest plantings and more especially, the Forestry Commission's heavy machinery, there is still enough left to see the original line in places. While following it from the remains of the above-noted culvert, I crossed into a field where the road was quite apparent and found another culvert on the same line but this time grass-covered and presumably still there. Beside it was a Roman fort that I went over several times with divining rods to convince myself.

In fact it was in a logical place to counter-balance the fort at Raeburnfoot 13kms away across the Craik Moor. At some period of the Roman occupations, there was the need for guard/patrol posts to provide escorts for travellers over wild moorland or hilly ground. In the Borders, this pattern can be seen on the Cheviots and with the Oxton fort on the south side of the Soutra hills.

The Craik fort is approximately 60m by 40m with its internal corners at **NT 34853 08088, 34828 08061, 34777 08103** and **34819 08124**. It is double-ditched on the east, west and north sides but single ditched on the south side which faces the road. Each gateway has ten postholes, suggesting a fighting platform arrangement similar to the gates at the Oakwood fort. This may mean that Craik fort was occupied during the same period, c AD 80 – c105.

An annexe on the north side is about 60m square and is single ditched. On the west side of the fort a small annexe stretches from the gateway south to the line of rampart of the main fort. This is also single ditched. Divining rods suggest that there are three Roman altars in this ditch but this might be stretching belief to breaking point

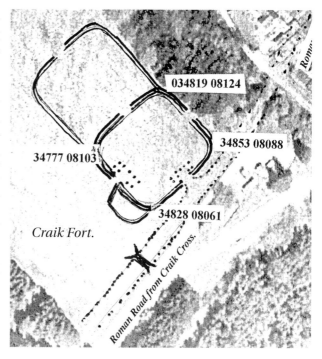

Craik Fort.

Although this fort does not show on any of the few air-photos, it would be quite easy to prove by putting one or two small trenches across one of the outer ditches.

As might be expected, there are two or more temporary camps in the flat haughs to the east of the fort. One that I measured was 100m by 80m and had the usual lines of rubbish pits 6m apart and 8m between the lines. The three corners available for plotting were at **NT 35028 08283, 35062 08202** and **34991 08144**. The other corner was in a private garden. On a dry year, this site would repay air photos.

Although the road was detectable in small sections between Craik and Groundistone Heights, it was more apparent at Hall Moss **NT 490 197**, where a series of rectangular raised platforms are beside an enclosure with four post holes in a 3.5m square. Being on

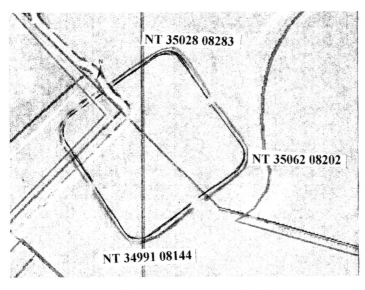

NT 35028 08283

NT 35062 08202

NT 34991 08144

Temporary camp at Craik

the top of the hill, this has to be a watch tower.

From here, the next 5kms are on the nearly straight line marked 'Drove Road' on the map. At Black Craig, **NT 508 212**, the rock shows signs of being ancient quarry, i.e., the rock has been dug into and the debris carried out rather than being taken away by wheeled carts. About 200m further along, a line of quarry pits appear on the south side of the road. These are still 1m deep and one is a double pit.

A POTENTIAL 'WATCH LINE' THROUGH THE BORDERS

In 1995, while tracing the east/west road from Craik to where it crosses the Scottish/English border at **NT 797 374**, I found that there a number of what seemed to be fortlets or watch/signal towers along the line of road. When I put the proposition that this might be a 'limes' or frontier line similar to the Gask Ridge, to Dr David Woolliscroft who was, and is, an authority on Roman frontiers and signalling, he was not dismissive of the idea and said that *'you are not suggesting anything implausible'*. This was encouraging and I carried on divining and plotting locations. He did point out that it might be a 'fortified interior road', similar to the one between the forts of Brough and Bowes on the borders of Cumbria and Durham. (David Woolliscroft usually answers letters, a talent almost unique among archaeologists.)

During that period, I walked and mapped most of the line of road and some of the fortlet/signal/watch tower sites. Fraser Hunter did take time to view some of the road but suggested that the verdict was still 'not proven. Nobody else was interested enough to reply to my letters and maps so I gave up, but always kept in mind the possibility of a Gask Ridge-type development through the Borders.

In August/September 2011, re-walked the line from Maxton to Groundistone Heights. By now I was more experienced, had a little more time and had acquired a GPS to give more accurate map references. I chose this section of road because the ground varies from arable land at Maxton to the hills at Groundistone and I wanted to re-check what I had found sixteen years ago to see if my ideas held up.

With the advantage of being able to find former postholes, I can say with conviction that there are ten watchtowers of similar size in the eighteen kilometers covered. Outside the body of the watchtowers, there was a larger enclosure made by a post-palisade with a slight ditch in front.

At each tower, several small buildings about 8m by 4m can be found beside the line of the road. Close to most of the towers, divining rods picked out small square or rectangular enclosures with rampart and two ditches. These I had previously marked down as fortlets but they do not have the regular planning of those on Dere Street so I have settled for calling them 'enclosed settlements'.

The placement of the towers is interesting and logical. All are on raised ridges or hillocks and many commanded a complete three hundred and sixty degree view. Most are visible to four or five neighbouring towers as well as Eildon Hill North and Ruberslaw, both of which have known signal stations. Northwards and eastwards, there were views of twenty to thirty miles. As a corporate identity, the towers could see the whole of the eastern Borders from the Forth to the Cheviots.

1. Maxton. NT 61506 30216. This tower is beside fort and a fortlet which formed the basis for a settlement that has produced 1st to 5th century Roman coins, Early Historic artifacts including a piece of Viking silver and medieval coins and pottery.

2. Wellrig. NT 60134 28943. This tower faces the broad straight road which is certainly of Roman origin. The modern day crossroads is on the same position as the crossroads of Dere Street and the Craik/Tweedmouth road of Roman times.

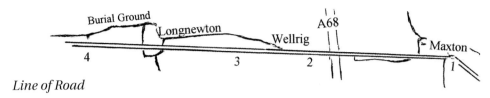

Line of Road

3. Greenend. NT 59330 28010. Tower sits in a wood about 30m south of the line of the Roman road.

4. Longnewton Mill. NT 57647 26772. Tower on hillock with road on south. There is an enclosed settlement to the east of the tower and several houses on both sides of the road.

5. Mire Hill. NT 56218 24832. This tower is beside No 19 in the Inventory of Roxburghshire which describes the site as being of an irregular shape 270 feet by 200 feet and *'mutilated to an extent –first by cultivation and later by the felling of a plantation – that it can only be classed as a site and its date and purpose uncertain'.* Since that publication, it has also been used as a dump for field stone-gathering.

In fact it is a rectangular fort, measuring approximately 100m by 75m, with a gateway in the middle of each side. The south gate faces the Roman road and is about 5.5m while the other three are about 3.5m. This is the size and shape of a Roman fort. On the north edge of the fort, there is a 3.5m square with a post in each corner which I am happy to claim as a watch tower.

6. Greenhouse. NT 55793 23969. Tower sits on edge of road with several 8 x 4m houses on both sides.

7. Cotfield 1. NT 53635 23028. Tower sits on edge of road with houses on both sides.

The road here is a raised mound and continues to be visible until No 10 at Groundistone.

8. Cotfield 2. NT 52300 22367. The tower is on the south side of the Roman road which is quite visible here and is marked on maps as a long straight 'Drove Road'. On the north side of the road, there is an enclosed settlement of 36m by 25m in a felled wood.

9. Black Craig. There is a tower at **NT 50580 20891** and an enclosed settlement roughly 15m square at **NT 50840 21317**; both are approx 50m from the road The line of road is very plain here with quarry pits at **NT 50677 21148** and the quarry at **NT 50677 21148** has no entrance for wheeled traffic.

10. Groundistone. Tower at **NT 49091 19708.** This is on the corner of an enclosure about 35m square which is within another approximately 180m by 120m. A number of raised platforms lie to the east of the site.

Spacing. The distances between the watch towers varied according to ground undulations and lines of sight. The measures are approximate but as near as I can get them.

Maxton to Well Rig	2100m		Greenhouse to Cotfield 1	2400m
Well Rig to Greenend	1300m		Cotfield 1 to Cotfield 2	1600m
Greenend to Longnewton Mill	2200m		Cotfield 2 to Black Craig	2100m
Longnewton Mill to Mire Hill	2400m		Black Craig to Groundistone	2200m
Mire Hill to Greenhouse	1000m			

The main purpose of these structures would be as watch towers with the ability to signal quickly through the area and backwards to Hadrian's Wall. This was not a defensive frontier with a post-wall such as runs the length of the German limes but rather a watch and report line.

The presence of houses beside the towers suggests that these were small settlements occupied by permanent garrisons who lived on site with their families. They could be the 'limitanei' (or borderers) who lived beyond the Roman province and kept watch for hostile forces approaching from the north or to give warning of trouble brewing within the area. If my suppositions are correct, the watch line is likely to have been in operation in the third and fourth centuries.

MAXTON

In 1965, Professor St Joseph found a Roman temporary camp at Maxton in Roxburghshire. His air photograph shows two sides with a rounded corner joining them.

In the years since, Roman artefacts and coins from the 1st to the 4th centuries AD have been found in the area by metal detectorists, suggesting there was either a permanent fort or large settlement on the site of the present village.

While walking the line of the Craik to Tweedmouth road, I found that it passed the village immediately south of the village and the north/south Dere Street is 1km to the west. These two roads intersect at **NT 604 290**.

Investigation revealed a double ditched Roman fort in the west end of the village and a smaller double ditched fortlet in the field to the north, a watch tower to the east and two temporary camps to the north/east. There are almost certainly further camps to the east but this area is still to be investigated.

The finds of miniature and broken bronze objects from what would have been a boggy piece of ground beside the Roman road, gives indications of ritual deposits. A miniature late Bronze Age axe, presently in Halliwell House Museum, Selkirk, suggests that late Bronze Age and the Roman Iron Age were more or less contemporary in the Borders.

Continuing the Craik/Tweedmouth road eastwards from Maxton, it crosses the River Teviot at Roxburgh Castle where a series of natural rock formations on the river bed would have provided a sound base for a bridge. In the King's Haugh, a flat field opposite the impressive mound of Roxburgh Castle, more than three hundred Roman coins from 1st century BC to 5th century AD have been found. These were spread over an area of a square kilometre on Springwood Park farm.

Most finds were from the King's Haugh but were segregated within the field. Those of the 1st/2nd century coins were found in an area of around 80m by 60m, in front of the

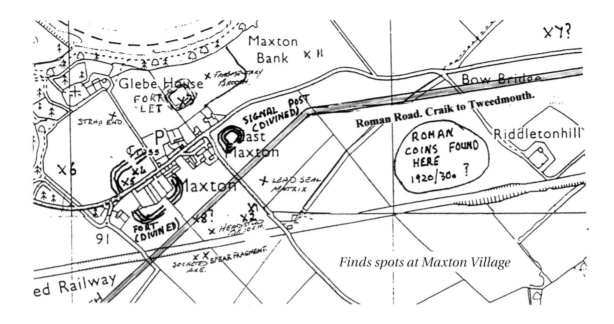

Finds spots at Maxton Village

Victorian Mausoleum and the later coins were spread along the side of the road that ran for about 200m along the bottom of the bank before turning to mount the higher ridge to the south. Curiously, no 1st/2nd coins were found in the 3rd/4th findspots and vice-versa.

Finding so many coins from all phases of Roman occupation of the Borders and for two centuries after the Roman army left, infers that there was a market or commercial trading place at the juncture of the Tweed and Teviot. This expanded into the Burgh of Roxburgh, the largest town in Scotland in medieval times and an international trading centre.

In Roman times, I suspect that there would be a quay where river boats could load and unload their goods.

Unusually, no Roman pottery or glass has been found on the site despite much searching but it is likely that the Roxburgh Castle mound would be the fort of a Votadinian chief who was 'approved of' by the occupying Romans i.e. Romanitas at work. Selkirkshire Book One gives a list of the coins found in this area and my idea is that there was a monetary economy still being in use long after the Roman troops had left the Borders. When I voiced this theory, it did my reputation as a normal if somewhat dull person, no good whatsoever.

The road continues down the south bank of the Tweed, passes Sprouston where Roman coins from 1st century BC to late 4th century AD have been found together with Samian pottery. It proceeds to Tweedmouth where everybody knows there must have been a Roman port and settlement – but nobody has found it yet. Memo to self: must do something about that if Ah'm spared.

TRIMONTIUM TO LYNE

The road is described in Selkirkshire Book One on pages 155 to 157 and I have found nothing new along the first section. The cover picture shows part of the road as it crosses Torwoodlee Mains farm. It is quite visible as it passes on the south side of Whytbank farm where the farmer used to complain about large stones being turned up every time the field was ploughed. A track branches off at a right angle, suggesting that a Roman fort or settlement may lie under the modern farm.

The road shows on air photographs crossing the Laidlawstiel fields and into Peeblesshire where it disappears from sight until re-appearing at Innerleithen.

The Innerleithen Camp Complex. I have always been aware that Innerleithen was a pivotal point of an early road system in the Upper Middle Tweed. As the river banks were the first pathways, the Tweed provided an east-west route; Leithen Water, Glentress Burn and the Dewar Burn gives a road through the Leithen Water Hills to the north, while the Quair Burn and its continuation, the Paddock Burn, give access to the Yarrow Valley on the south.

So it is logical that any occupying army would place a permanent force there to police the area. Yet, apart from the two mentions of a temporary camp, the site appears in none of the many books on Roman Scotland and only as a dot on the Map of Roman Britain.

The Inventory of Peeblesshire No 373 states that *'Crop marks on air photographs show part of the ditch of a temporary camp on the level ground between Innerleithen Railway Station and the river Tweed. About 340ft of the N. side, the rounded NW corner and 840ft of the W. side are visible and there is a gate 55ft wide in the later side some 550ft S. of the corner. The size of the camp is uncertain since the whole of the S. portion has been eroded away by the river, and no trace of the E. side can be seen on the photographs. The position of the surviving gateway suggests, however, that the camp cannot have measured less than 1000ft from N. to S.'*

Working on the theory that there is seldom only one Roman temporary camp on a site, I had a look at the area some years ago and was secure enough in my findings to write in SB1, *'The marching camp at Innerleithen has a double-ditched fortlet in the south-east corner.'* I was also able to determine that the report of the south portion of the camp being eroded in post-Roman times was wrong as there were at least three smaller temporary camps in the flat fields beside the river.

To give more gravitas to my investigation, I spent three days in July 2011 with GPS and divining rods stepping out the area and marking the sites. There was certainly a lot more Roman activity at the mouth of the Leithen Water than is noted in the Inventory of Peeblesshire or appears on the APs of the area. In fact there have been at least seven temporary camps on the site and one permanent fort. There may be many more under the Georgian/Victorian spread of houses and mills over the flatter ground to the south of the Main Street.

Given the location on a natural crossroads, this is not an unusually high number over the hundred years of intermittent occupation. Divining rods may not be the accepted proofs but they are very useful indicators for revealing what cannot be seen on the surface.

The fort is double ditched with a gate in the middle of each side and has the 'playing card' shape which was more common in the Antonine period. The south side of the fort is partially on the line of the largest temporary camp on the site and is mostly under tree cover Despite this, it can be determined that it is approximately 110 metres by 75 metres internally.

The wall base is 3 metres wide and the two ditches are each 4 metres across. This is a fairly standard smaller-sized fort.

In the outer ditch at the NW corner of the fort, there are two small altars (this is an act of faith) and a small annexe in the wood to the west of the fort. This contains up to ten buildings that are about 8 metres by 4.5 metres and a bathhouse south of the fort at **NT 33278 36005.**

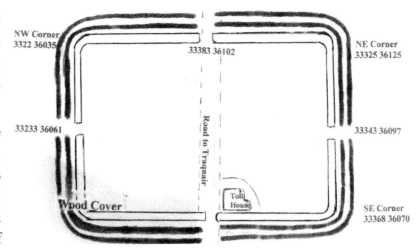

NW Corner 3322 36035

33383 36102

NE Corner 33325 36125

33233 36061

33343 36097

Road to Traquair

Wood Cover

Toll House

SE Corner 33368 36070

The Fort at NT 335 361

The Temporary Camps. While walking the fields around the lower parts of Innerleithen, I found that my sixty pace measurement appeared many times in the temporary camps. On stepping out sixty paces in rough grass several times and measuring the result, I reckoned that this was near enough to the Roman land measure, the 'actus' which was 120 Roman pedes, equal to 116.5 Imperial feet or 35.5 metres. A square actus was an 'actus quadratus', two of which together made an 'iugerum', a Roman acre of 240 pedes in length and 120 pedes in breadth, i.e., 28,800 square feet.

Pursuing the numerical equation on the field, I noted that the gateways in the camps were five of my paces or a twelfth of an actus. The short barrier wall or 'titulus' was ten paces in front of the gateway and this was usually ten paces in length, these being a 'uncia agri'. This knowledge was to come in useful.

While looking at the temporary camps, I always checked that they had rows of rubbish pits with their adjoining tent-pole pits to prove that they were temporary camps rather than fields although there is no reason why they should have been both at different times.

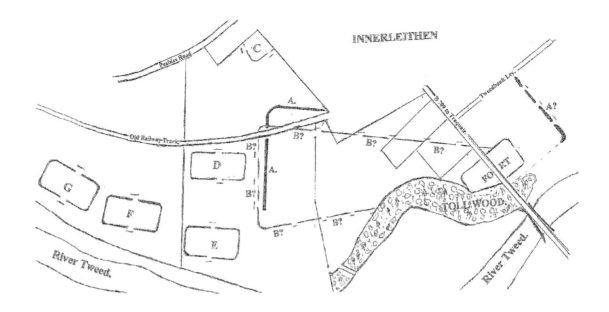

Camp A. I found the camp noted in the Peeblesshire Inventory quite easily although there are no visible signs at ground level. Both ditch and rampart are broader than any of the other camps in the immediate area, so I decided that this must have had a comparatively long term occupation, probably a summer campaign during the Agricolan period. I could not find the 55ft wide gate or the claim that the southern half of the west side had been eroded in the post-Roman period.

Most of this camp is under Victorian and modern development but I did get a corner at **NT 33433 36125** and gates at **33403 36159, 33373 36203** and **33343 36238**. These could be part of the east side of the first camp on the site. However variations on the west side of the camp confirm that there had been more than one on the same location.

Camp B. This is a puzzler as it deviates from the standard rectangular Roman camp and bisects the proposed area of Camp A diagonally from corner to corner. Starting at the NE corner of the fort, the ditch runs to **NT 32847 36211**. This line has four gateways at sixty pace intervals, each with a titulus in front.

It then turns at a right angle to run the line of Camp A's west side to **NT 32843 35994**. This line of ditch contains three gateways at sixty pace intervals and tituli in front. Turning again, it makes for the NW corner of the fort. This line has four gateways in the open fields and another in the Toll Wood.

Camp C. This is a smaller camp with only the SW corner and two gateways detectable before vanishing under modern housing beside the Peebles Road.

Camps D, E, F, G – The Iugerum. West of the main camp complex and the fort, were four camps of an identical size if an allowance was made for slight variations in my pacing. These were 120 paces by 60 paces which I worked out as an 'iugerum' or Roman acre. Three of the camps were on the low fields beside the river which contradicts the theory that this was scooped away in post-Roman times; the fourth was on the raised bank back from the river.

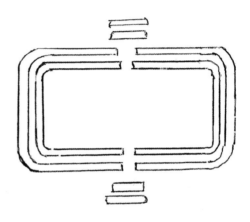

Illustration of Iugerum

The one unusual feature of these camps was that, although they were a rectangular shoe-box shape within a rampart and ditch enclosure, there were only two gates and these were in the middle of the long sides with tituli in front. Thinking they might simply be fields, I subjected them to the rubbish pit/tent-pole tests and confirmed that at some stage, they had been used as temporary camps.

Rather than taking up space with unnecessary figures, I will give the corner locations according to my GPS but it must be remembered that these give a decree of variation in positioning whereas divining rods are accurate to within 30cms.

Camp D. **32783 36126, 32694 36171, 32690 36126, 32781 36123.**
Camp E. **32748 36004, 32738 35957, 32647 35978, 32652 36024.**

Camp F. **32623 36065, 32602 36031, 32538 36083, 32546 36157.**

Camp G. **32520 36194, 32478 36192, 32422 36292, 32436 36358.**

Some weeks after the original survey, I went back to have another look at these unusual shapes. Careful examination discovered that there were twelve tent sites in each half of the enclosure. They were in rows 8m apart with tents at 6m intervals; this is what I had come to expect in tented temporary camps.

I reckoned that twelve tents would house a 'century' which, despite is name, was usually around 80 men under the command of a centurion. So it would be fitting that these unusually shaped camps could each be the temporary quarters for two centurions and their men.

With 80 men tented within an actus quadratus, this became the standard 'building block' of the Roman temporary camp. It also explains why I keep finding camps that have actus long sections (35.5m) of rampart and ditch between each gate. With a road running from one gate to one on the opposite side, this effectively made a chess-board pattern within the camp. So a camp with three gates on the long sides and two gates on the shorter sides would have twelve individual actus quadrati and thus able to house twelve centuries, probably around 960 men. This size of camp would be about 4.2 acres which would allow 228 men to the acre. Polybius, a 1st century Greek historian, reckons on 240 men to the acre, the Rey Cross figures give about 300 while others have a guesstimate of up to 480. So I think that the 'Innerleithen Measure' is fairly accurate.

The century having its own space would implement the bonding which has been encouraged in all fighting forces since the beginning of time.

Like all my other divining discoveries, proof awaits excavation or more sophisticated geophysics readings than we have at present, but there was one bonus point on the Innerleithen searches. While looking round the area for Roman temporary camps, I found a grave on the top of a glacial mound at **NT32872 3591**. As the camps lines respected this, it could be either Roman or pre-Roman. It would be easy to dig too.

And there again I might be wrong on all propositions stated, but not on the fact that they are there.

Chapelhill Farm, Peebles. In 1995, a metal detectorist brought in a bag of 'junk' which he had found on the field beside the road between Chapelhill Farm and the town of Peebles. Amongst this was a 5th century Anglo-Saxon stylus.

This was a site which I thought had possibilities because of its location, but it took until 2008 before I got round to doing something about it; in fact I was looking for proof of a Christian chapel to fit in with the academically-accepted theory that Peebles was a notable centre of worship in the early Christian period.

Using divining rods, I didn't find evidence of a Christian chapel but did find the shape of a rampart and double ditched enclosure 70m by 50m with gateways in the centre of each side. The shape and location were right for a Roman fort and it passed the bathhouse/latrine test with two bathhouses and a latrine in the annexe, so I put some time into

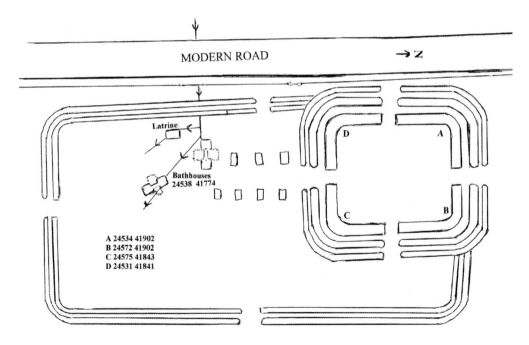

mapping it out. The inside corners of the fort are marked and, if the divining rods are truthful, there are two altars in the northwest corner of the fort.

This is inside a larger enclosure which might originally have been a temporary camp but had been made into an annexe for the fort. A road leading out of the south gate has buildings on each side; these are 5/6m by 4m.

There may be two separate occupations and the whole idea has still to be proved by air photographs at the Royal Commission or by putting two or three trial trenches across the ditches if the farmer is agreeable.

Peebles. On land configuration alone and the fact that it stands at a natural point of intersection of routes, I had long considered that the Old Town would have been an ideal site for a Roman permanent fort. Certainly there was an early settlement there with 5th/6th century Christian-inscribed stones and it was tempting to make a comparison with the Early Christian Old Melrose and its adjoining Trimontium fort.

This was a totally wrong assumption. It is a point of intersection of routes at the present day but in the 1st and 2nd centuries, the Roman surveyors looped their road round the site of Peebles to avoid the hills of Venlaw, Janet's Brae and the Neidpath heights above Jedderfield. This made the road run immediately to the south of the Chapelhill fort before it went over the hill to the Hallyne Roman complex.

That route left the site that is now Peebles isolated on two sides by hills with the Tweed on the third side, making it very suitable for an Early Christian holy place. For their faith, the early monks liked their 'diseart' (or desert) away from the common herd in order to worship in peace but for economics, preferred to have a convenient road for pilgrims close by. The comparison to Old Melrose was not too far out.

CHAPTER EIGHT

The Hallyne Complex – Another Trimontium?

There is an east/west Roman road which joins Trimontium on Dere Street with Castledykes on the Nithsdale/Clydesdale road. Both forts held pivotal permanent garrisons during the phases of the Roman occupation of southern Scotland. On the road between them is the Hallyne Roman complex.

The village of Hallyne lying 7kms west of Peebles, has a concentration of Roman occupation with two permanent forts, two fortlets, a number of temporary camps and at least three signal/watch towers. Collectively they provide a focal point to the Roman presence in central southern Scotland.

EASTER HAPPREW FORT

This fort was accidently discovered in air photographs taken by the RAF in 1955 and partly excavated the following year to see how it fitted into the accepted pattern of Roman occupation. The site was well chosen, being on a high glacial plateau beside the meeting-place of four natural routes through the hills. In the ten day excavation, enough evidence was collected to be reasonably certain that the occupation was of short duration, probably from AD 80-86 or at the latest AD 103 when the withdrawal of a legion was responsible for Trimontium and Oakwood being abandoned. After excavation, the fort site was taken into the protective care of R.C.A.H.M.S.

In 1995, local detectorists, Paul and Brenda Smith decided to detect on the distinctly uninspiring flat fields lying to the east and south of the higher fort site. When they brought their finds to me for identification and confirmation, I was amazed at the number and quality of their finds for this was not field-spread from the fort. The first 'take' consisted of a republican denarius and eight copper coins, mainly of Vespasian; in bronze - a bell a terret, a ring, a horse's head and neck with Roman harness, two broken handles and more broken and melted pieces; and in lead - three Roman scale weights and one plumb weight. Melted bronze scrap showed that casting was being done on site and the number of Roman weights indicated that this was a prominent trading centre.

While the detectorists continued to search the lower fields, I walked the fort site and its annexes looking for non-metallic finds. At the same time, I was divining the flat area where the bulk of the finds were being made. It measured around 400m by 250m and was overlooked by higher ground on three sides with no sign of defensive wall or ditch.

I made out that there was a main road running through the site and on each side of this there were lines of uniform buildings measuring about 8/9m long by 4m wide which ran parallel to the road. I never thought to make a rough sketch of the site and it was some years after that I realised that this could be a civilian settlement which would not necessarily have anything to do with the fort.

Two years later, one of the fields was in turnips with sheep eating them from the ground. After a particularly wet spell and a lot of sheep tramping around, the rectangular outlines of the buildings could be seen. These suggested that they were the stone bases of sleeper-beam buildings similar to those in the south annexe of the Trimontium fort.

When the finds from Easter Happrew were evaluated, Fraser Hunter would write *'Given the location in a non-defensive position, there seems little doubt that the finds derive from an extensive vicus or civilian settlement outside the fort. Its condition is frequently good, implying that it is not manuring spread, rubbish disposal from the fort or some similar process. This is of considerable importance as vicus sites, while originally a feature of most if not all forts, have rarely been investigated in Scotland.......It is already clear that this is one of the richest surface collections known from a Scottish Roman site'.*

With the finds being all 1st century, I made a case for the population being transferred to Peebles Old Town which would have been a good site for settlement and it was an Early Christian centre. This was wrong and a much better suggestion was closer at hand.

LYNE FORT

I have visited Lyne Fort several times in the past but only started to take a closer interest when I was searching for Roman bathhouses in the Borders and a known Roman fort like Lyne was the ideal testing ground for my theories. The idea which I had previously used at Trimontium was to find the drain/pipe bringing water into the fort, trace it along its length and mark where it branched off to supply water-tanks, latrines, baths etc.

Lyne is the only recognised Roman fort in the Borders Region which is still visible on the ground. It was excavated in 1901 and again in 1959 – 63. On the strength of one piece of 1st century and a quantity of 2nd century pottery, the fort was dated with some reservations to having been occupied during both periods.

The visible fort has an area of 5.6 acres with annexes on the north and south sides. With a known fortlet to the immediate north, there seemed to be little that a plod with divining rods could add to the knowledge of the site other than to locate the site of the bathhouse. This was to prove a serious under-estimation.

The 1959-63 excavators came to the tentative conclusion that the garrison of Easter Happrew fort either moved across the river to build a new fort at Lyne around AD 86 or were recalled for service on the Continent a bit later. Whatever the reason, it would seem that the civilian population of the Easter Happrew settlement simply moved to a drier site beside the new road then being built.

There is another possible explanation. When the Roman troops were recalled from southern Scotland around AD 103, the people of the vicus could have simply upped sticks literally, and founded their own settlement on a better site across the river, staying put until the troops came back around AD 140 to build a fort there. The idea of a large civilian settlement without much military support is quite common in England and the rest of the Roman Empire but has not been seriously considered in a Scottish context.

While plodding along the water-track which ran into the fort from the north, I crossed two large ditches and a 6m thick wall-base which was 55m north of the present north rampart.

There were no obvious traces on the ground and only the faintest on any APs that I could find. When I traced the wall to the rounded corners and on to join the ramparts of the visible fort, I realised that the original fort had been reduced to its present dimensions. This gives additional credence to the theory that there had been two forts on the same site.

This reduction of the Lyne fort could correspond to one of the periods at Trimontium when the area of the fort was divided by building a stone wall leaving two thirds remaining as a military fort and the other third as a manufacturing complex.

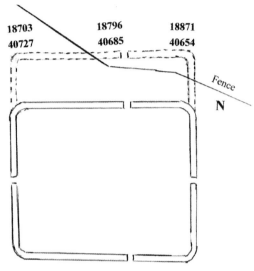

Lyne Fort Reduction

In the original construction of the Lyne fort, the north gate at **NT 18795 40685**, had seven posts on the outward face and six posts behind. I had observed this layout in the main gates of Pennymuir, Trimontium and Bonjedward.

> Reverting to my fencing experiences. If an ancient post-hole can be located by divining rods and the stump of the post extracted, this would provide material for dating by dendrochronology or carbon dating and pollen analysis to tell what the countryside was like at the time of construction. Excavation made easy!

In the excavations of 1959–1963, a large pit was found immediately behind the east rampart of the known fort. *'The top measured 14 feet by 8 feet. It was excavated to 13 feet below the present surface but abandoned when the sides showed signs of collapsing'.* As this was similar to some of the hundred plus pits at Trimontium, I divined behind the east rampart and found another eight of a similar size. Further investigation revealed a further twenty scattered inside the fort but these were 2.5m to 3m in top diameter.

THE ANNEXES

Roman forts are stereotyped, built to a regular pattern and in fact, quite dull except for the objects lost or left in the ground; the most interesting parts are in the annexes. There lived the family dependants, the traders, manufacturers and providers of services for the troops in the fort. They were usually enclosed by a rampart and single ditch which was territory-marking rather than defensive but this did not prevent other houses being built outside the annexes, usually along the line of road leading out the military settlement.

While at Lyne on the bathhouse search, I took the opportunity to try the rods over the annexes to see what was there. I used the map of Lyne in P.S.A.S, 1961–1962 as a master plan. Divining rods agreed with the size and location of the south annexe and found several buildings around 8m by 4m. These were in rows corresponding to those identified (but not mapped) at Easter Happrew.

There were some problems on the map of the north annexe. Neither excavation had been in a place to find that the north wall been moved 55m and this put things slightly out of kilter. What was recognised as a small annexe in the first excavation was extended by a *'hitherto unrecorded polygonal annexe recognised from an air photograph taken by Dr St Joseph'*. This photograph shows one gate in an unbroken dark line of ditch but my divining rods indicate a further three breaks in the wall. The reason for this would be that the ditch was continuous but there could be wooden bridges across it as required. This would allow drainage and prevent stagnant water building up in short stretches of ditch. The additional three extra gates could open up the enclosed area - for a market perhaps?

In this area, the rods detected a number of buildings, some quite large, which were hinted at in the above AP and rows of the 8m by 4m houses similar to those that appear in the south annexe. Some of these were built on the ground previously occupied by the northern part of the original fort.

At Lyne I found two legionary bathhouses with divining rods, one inside the north annexe and one outside in a square enclosure which was clipped by the enclosure wall and ditch. This showed that a change had taken place in the development of the site and this was confirmed by an AP of the site in PSAS 1961–1962.

EAST ANNEXE

The combined areas of the north and south annexes were sufficient to service the needs of the Lyne fort but there was an obvious case for expanding the search to the flat land on the east of the fort. A closer look at this area showed an extensive but unrecorded (as far as I know) east annexe which doubled the enclosed area. The dual tracks of an enclosing wall and ditch are visible on the ground and in air photographs. This runs along the top of the ridge but contrary to the useful explanation that 'it is something agricultural', no farmer would be stupid enough to put a drainage ditch along the edge of a steep escarpment. These dual marks show up well on Google Maps of the site.

The new addition is an extension of the south rampart and ditch of the south annexe. It runs along the ridge before turning north at **NT 18999 40393** and eventually joining up with the north-east corner of the extended north annexe at **NT 18960 40682**. There are four gateways in this length of enclosure wall and a potential watch tower. With this area enclosed, there was a blanket of annexes around the fort except on the west where the ground falls away steeply.

 This new annexe was to further complicate the site. During a later visit to determine the location/s of the bathhouse/s, I spent some time divining in the east annexe, finding rows of 8m x 4m buildings with doors facing each other in an orderly fashion across 6m wide streets. The buildings had 6m spaces between them and about 5m behind each building there was a pit whose surface measurement was 2.5m to 3m in diameter.

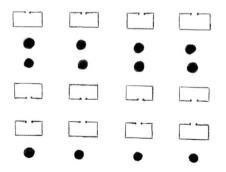

House plots and pits of the East Annexe

A day's divining in cold weather allowed me to walk out a plan in the snow. After marking out eight rows of houses and pits, it was obvious that these were houses in a planned development. The overall plan was not unlike the town expansion schemes of the 1920/30s or the 'Prefab' developments in the late 1940s.

The pits at each house plot would likely be soak-away pits for surface water or urine. They may have been used as rubbish pits but there would be very little rubbish to dispose of in the 2nd century settlement as anything usable would be re-cycled. The rich pits at Trimontium were filled during a hurried evacuation of the fort when anything unable to be carried off would be hidden in the pits.

> Pits are common in the annexes of Roman forts in the Borders and I don't know any which doesn't have pits within the annexe and along the road outside it. These and the drains leading into the fort for latrines, cisterns and baths are indicators where unrecorded forts lie.

A trip round the other two Lyne annexes, revealed the same pattern. Were they all planned and laid out at the same time? At Lyne they probably were; but a trip over to Easter Happrew revealed the same pattern of houses and pits. With the Easter Happrew vicus already dated to 1st century by finds, the first fort at Lyne or at least its surrounding settlement, could date from late 1st century or very early 2nd; or there again, maybe not.

Present knowledge has the Roman military forces withdrawn from southern Scotland in AD 103 and not return until AD 139/140. This would have left the planted romanised civilian population in a quandary. Did the vicus/town at Lyne survive the gap years as a trading settlement? This period is a crossword puzzle with most of the clues missing; we just don't know. We need more clues to even guess at the timescale but it would be a useful exercise to pass a number of friendly detectorists over the annexes of the fort to see if the finds from the vicus of Happrew are duplicated at Lyne.

The new annexe had not finished with its surprises. While plodding around where the road comes out from the east gate of the Lyne fort, I was confronted by a structure with a rampart and double ditches. Investigations revealed that these enclosed 27m square which held four barrack blocks 18m by 4m, two buildings 4m square and what has to be an oven against the wall. I recognised this construction from the fortlets along the line of Dere Street but finding it inside a built-up area was unusual. Its ditches ran parallel to those of the fort and respected the houses on the side of the road out of the east gate.

The problem was unlikely that anyone would contemplate an un-noted annexe with orderly rows of houses in it and even fewer would believe there could be a fortlet so close beside a fort. However, fortune favours the foolhardy as well as the brave. The Scottish Borders Council published a book 'Early Settlers in the Borders' in 1997 and Plate 6 is an air photograph of the Lyne Fort. Just outside the east gate on the south side of the exit road there are the faint but irrefutable rounded corners and ditches of a square Roman fortlet in the place where divining rods said it was. Photographic proof is especially welcome. I just hope that R.C.A.H.M.S. can come up with more definitive photographs.

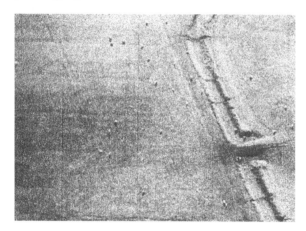

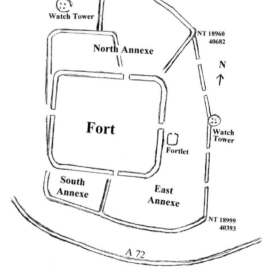

This leaves the plan of Lyne Fort looking something like this (right) but with still a lot of questions still to be answered.

LYNE TEMPORARY CAMPS

Air photographs reveal the cropmarks of one large temporary camp and one slightly smaller and less definite to the east of Lyne farm. Ground experience has shown me that the Romans made frequent use of good sites when moving troops across the country. Using divining rods I got so many walls, ditches and titula that I gave up after three days and illustrate only those lines of which I am positive.

Camp A is the one delineated by air photographs. It is there and is certain although there are more gates than are visible.

Camp B is slightly larger. Although I have left out the gateways, they appear every sixty of my paces (an actus) and each has a titulus in front of it. Where the line of wall crosses the small burn beside the farm road, there are two lines of posts at 3.5m spacings. This suggests that there was either a raised walkway to level the two sides of the burn or that this was a wooden barrier to stop infiltrators; or perhaps both.

In both of the above, there was a confusion of walls, ditches and corners. **Camp C** was complete and to a more standard design. **Camps D** and **E** were complete with gateways every actus and tituli placed at 10m in front. I found that this is a standard placing in temporary camps.

Rather surprisingly, there was a signal station on the top of a mound at **NT 20176 40621**. The site was good for viewing but this is unusual for temporary camps so there may be another fortlet in the vicinity.

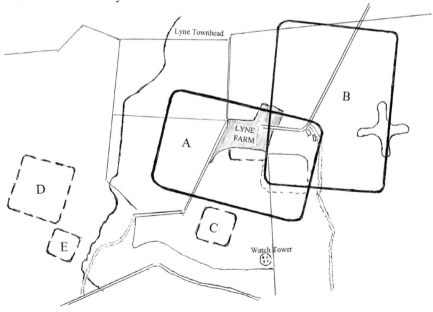

PROOFS AND TO BE PROVED

I have been making a case that the Hallyne complex of Roman Forts should be placed on an almost equal footing to Trimontium and Castledykes. Trimontium has had a hundred years of time, money and interest spent in unravelling its story; Castledykes has not had the same concentration of interest but has a good record of Roman activity. The Hallyne complex lies halfway along the main east/west road which joins the two and lies at a natural crossroads.

As well as the east/west road, a Roman road left Lyne fort east gate and headed north. I traced this to above Eddleston, meaning to come back and continue until I found definite traces of Roman military occupation.

In 2010, members of the Peeblesshire Archaeological Society came up with photographs of a rectangular shape at Darnhall, north of Eddleston. It did have the appearance of a normal Roman marching camp and divining rods gave a pattern showing three gateways along the long sides and two on the short sides with a titulus in front of each gateway. Inside the camp, the rubbish pits conformed to the usual pattern.

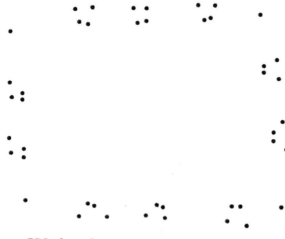

GPS plan of gateway and tituli at Darnhall

By marking out the camp corners, the posts at each gateway and the ends of the tituli, we got a fairly convincing plan of a marching camp but when enthusiastic members dug a few trial pits, no positive evidence was forthcoming. However, as I found lines of rubbish pits and tent-pole holes within a rampart and ditch perimeter, I am still reasonably certain that a Roman marching camp will show up on this site some day.

Proofs. These are meagre but compelling. The metal-detecting activities of Paul and Brenda Smith revealed a rich settlement at Easter Happrew which has no enclosure ties with fort above. Although yet to be proven by conventional means, the large independent settlement laid out on a grid pattern was unlikely to be done by other than Roman agrimensores.

The Easter Happrew fort is postulated to be the 'Carbantorigum' of Ptolemy and 'Carbantium' in the Ravenna Cosmography. Both mean a 'wagon-ford, or chariot-ford'. This is probably right as it lies roughly to the west of Trimontium in a corrected Ptolemy map and the first Roman road did ford the river near the site. This reasoning is strengthened by the two Roman bronze horse-head chariot ornaments, a pendant ornament for attaching to a phalera and terrets found on the site by metal-detectorists.

The Lyne east annexe is attached to the fort by an enclosure wall which can be seen on the ground and in APs. In the annexe, an air photograph by the Borders Regional archaeologist shows a fortlet where, frankly, no fortlet should be.

Two legionary bathhouses show up on Cambridge University APs of the site, one within the extended north annexe enclosure and one outside but clipped by the enclosure ditch. These have been un-noted in archaeological record

To be Proved. The first thing to be looked at is the extent of the settlement at Easter Happrew and the annexes at Lyne. Sleeper-beam buildings do not show up well in geophysics but rows of pits could be found by ground-penetrating radar. Most of the best finds from Trimontium came from pits. In theory, the furnaces of the bathhouses in the annexes and fort at Lyne should have left a heat footprint for a magnetometer to find.

Excavation would prove much but it is expensive, time-consuming and unlikely.

IS IT WORTH IT?

Given the fact that the two (still to be proven) settlements are far larger than was required to service two quite small Roman forts of different dates, the question is why?

Finds from the Easter Happrew civilian settlement indicate that it had an already romanised population around AD 80. After a few years the people of the settlement had moved away but the similarity of design makes it unlikely to be anywhere else than the Lyne fort site.

My theory is that in the first few years of occupation, the Roman authorities were designing a planned province with a planted population, the first centre being at Easter Happrew and then at Lyne. There is evidence that a similar plan was used at some period to divide up the land along the roadsides into uniform patterns of small holdings. This is examined in Chapter Ten.

CHAPTER NINE

Berwickshire and Teviotdale

BERWICKSHIRE

Berwickshire has long been considered to have no Roman remains *'because the Votadini who held the area were friendly to the Romans, so there was no need to site a fort there.'* This is not exactly true. It is just that there are no obvious remains like the Lyne Fort and nobody has thought to look for traces of their presence.

Richard Strathie has been a great help over the years in my search for archaeological sites and, more importantly, for proving them. As well as being a computer programmer, he flew a microlite aircraft and could take photographs at the same time. Then based at Gattonside, he could be flying very quickly if the conditions on the ground were right. This is a bonus to an earth-bound fieldwalker

While flying over Greenlaw, he took a couple of photos of the known promontory fort at Greenlaw Dean in 1998 and they were so clear that he used one as a screensaver on his computer. It was while we were chatting years later that I noticed the straight sides and rounded corners of a potential Roman camp on the screen. For the rest of that year (2006), I spent spare time at Greenlawdean with divining rods and came across a number of interesting shapes in the ground, some visible, some not. On reporting them to the appropriate authorities then, I received little encouragement.

In the time between the photograph being taken and 2006, most of the potential camp area had been planted with spruce trees and had clumps of willow-herb growing amongst them. Crawling in and out of these made accurate measuring impossible and paced measurements are even more approximate. Flies, clegs, midges and heat were further impediments. Since then, a portion of the site has been cleared of trees and restored to grass so it would be a good time to re-assess the site.

For the record. On Greenlawdean Farm, near where Herrit's Dyke crosses the Blackadder Water, there is a camp complex with at least two temporary camps and one permanent fort with an annexe at **NT 694 479**.

The large outer camp, here shown by pointers, is approximately 300m by 250m with single rampart, c 3m at base and a ditch 5m wide. It would be interesting to go back now to divine this wall for gateways.

Inside this, is a smaller temporary camp of which I could only divine c 200m of the north side and part of the east side as far as the gateway. The rampart and ditch were similar to the above but the three gates each had the double claviculae defences similar to those of the temporary camp at Oakwood.

Inside the temporary camps, there is a permanent fort measuring 120m by 80m with a small annexe on the west side. The rampart-base was 4m thick and two ditches 5m and 3.5m. The three gates which I could get to had four posts on each side of the gate suggesting either a platform over the entrance or guard houses.

The annexe leading out from the west gate was about 50m square and was enclosed by a 3m rampart and a single 4m ditch. There were at least eight rectangular buildings at right angles to the road.

To the north of this complex there are a number of temporary camps with single ditches and walls and a probable fortlet. This area needs a lot of divining yet.

On the flats beside the Langrist Burn, here seen on the left of the above picture, there are some interesting mounds of tumbled local red sandstone. At least three slight mounds indicated buildings with walls 30cms thick and right-angled corners. I did plan out one of them and suggest that it was a bathhouse. This was to give a start to my bathhouse search through the Borders.

To the north at **NT 693 483**, there are two very visible enclosures approx 250m by 280m. The wall mounds are 5m wide and still more than 1m high with a 1m deep ditch on the outside. Both have two 5m gateways near one corner with an occasional 2m gap in other places so they are not a standard Roman fort pattern. They are not wood enclosures, ancient or modern and I can think of no useful agricultural purpose for any period. Certainly they are beside Herrit's Dyke and may be associated with it. But is Herrit's Dyke of the pre-Roman, Roman or Early Historic period?

Inside one enclosure is a (divined) large building approx 70m long and 7m wide with wings approx 35m by 7m at right angles to the main body. Part of this is visible on air photographs belonging to the Estate. If this shape was found in the south of England, there would no hesitation in pronouncing it was a 'villa farm'. Is there any reason why there should not be a Romano-British villa farm in Berwickshire?

On the other side of the Blackadder from the Greenlawdean complex, a recorded earthwork at **NT 692 472** (Berwickshire No 340) appears on an early map as 'Station'. This was worth investigating as there was nothing to explain the name.

I did find a Roman watch tower at **NT 69631 46881** and a fortlet at **NT 69570 46737**. The fortlet was 20m square with rampart and two ditches. The gateway was facing east. It had an annexe 50m by 40m with a small bathhouse and latrine in the south west corner. This was the same pattern as I had found on Dere Street.

Knowing that one tower would lead to another, I found this 3kms distant at **NT 71347 44531** along the ridge near Old Greenlaw. This was in a wood beside a 1940 outlook post which had been utilised by a family of badgers. The garrisoning 20m square fortlet was at **NT 71250 44637** with a small bathhouse and latrine in the lower ground at **NT 71165 44749.**

Both towers command wide views over the surrounding countryside and while two towers do not make a defensive line, they give an indication on where to look.

More potential for discovery on APs is a mound situated at the west end of Greenlaw. at **NT 70483 46125** where divining rods indicated a small Roman fort 60m by 45m with rampart and double ditches. A large annexe approximately 90m by 140m lay on the east side and a small one 60m by 50m on the north which contained the bathhouse and latrine. Like many Roman forts it is situated at a point where early roads would meet. No identifiably Roman finds were made during a field-walk but a metal detect over the site could pay dividends.

Berwickshire needs a lot of investigation. An extension of The Devil's Causeway crosses the Tweed near the modern A1 bridge and on to Ayton etc. This was the logical first route for the legions to march into Scotland while being supported by an offshore fleet.

TEVIOTDALE

Teviotdale was one of the most obvious places to look for a Roman road with two forts at Bonjedward in the lower end of the valley and the temporary camps at Cavers Mains and Eastcote near Denholm at the other.

Looking at the countryside near Denholm, the most appealing place for a Roman fort seemed to be a wooded knowe at Ashybank Farm. And there was a small double-ditched fort about 60m by 45m with an annexe to the east. Part of the fort was within the wood, as was a signal tower. The bathhouse was 200m to the north-east and of the usual pattern.

As I had found a series of forts at Bonjedward and a small double-ditched fort with attached annexe at Cavers **NT 54936 17373,** I thought it likely that there would be one in between.

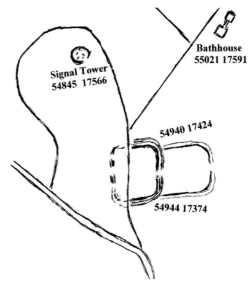

Signal Tower
54845 17566

Bathhouse
55021 17591

54940 17424

54944 17374

From Ancrum Bridge westward, the Roman road lies under the modern one for most of the next 5km. On the south side of road at Lanton Mains, a nice flat-topped mound looked an ideal situation for a fort, and it was.

The original double-ditched fort was about 90m by 70m and had been extended by another 30m, again double-ditched before having a further single-ditched annexe added. East of the fort was a hollow where I found a

Small fort at Roughhopes Plantation

strangely-shaped building, the like of which I had only seen once six years previously at Greenlawdean and had tentatively identified as a Roman bathhouse. A later return to

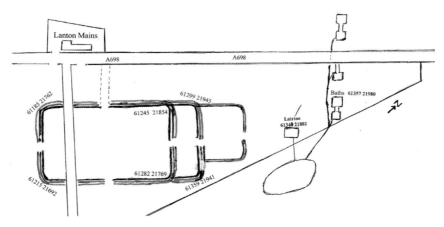

Lanton Mains

A698   A698

61185 21762

61299 21945

61245 21854

Baths 61357 21980

Latrine
61340 21881

61282 21769

61215 21692

61359 21941

this site with more experience added another two bathhouses and a latrine to the plan. The watch tower was at **NT 61457 21675**.

A fort of this size meant that there had to be a temporary camp to accommodate the troops building it and this was in the field immediately to the south-east of the fort. It was 120 paces by 60 paces which is the Roman acre or 'iugerum' and had the distinctive tent measurements in it.

In 1995, Billy Butler, detectorist extraordinaire, handed in a denarius of Vespasian for recording. This he had found 'at Lanton' on the site I am claiming for a Roman fort

There is still a lot more work to be done on this line of road.

CHAPTER TEN

The Countryside - A Colonia?

Studies of the Romans in Scotland have always concentrated on the military aspects of life. Forts, fortlets, annexes, transit and temporary camps and roads can be seen, investigated and placed into their military context. Archaeological thought tends to concentrate on what can be seen on the ground, found in the ground or photographed from the air and only those are considered worthy of further investigation and excavation.

The impression that this gives is that the southern part of what is now Scotland was one large military establishment with life existing only within or near the forts. Even finds from fort annexes are usually considered as part of the supply chain for the army. Items like children and women's shoes are identified as belonging to soldiers' families and they are likely to be so.

But this gives a very one-sided view of the Roman period in southern Scotland. The increasing use of metal detectors shows that Roman influence extended across the area and into some of the more inaccessible parts of the region. This rather contradicts the idea that the comparatively brief periods of Roman occupation would have no effect on the native peoples although the discovery of one Roman coin or brooch may not indicate a massive change in lifestyle. What would be very useful would be a pottery detector because Samian pottery is looked on as the essential ingredient for civilized living. In fact there is very little to be found outside the larger established military forts.

More positive indications are the changes in building techniques when the customary roundhouse gave way to rectangular buildings. This was not universal throughout the Borders and is difficult to prove as roundhouse interest and excavation tended to be complete with the publication of the Inventories of the respective counties in the 1950s.

However in 1998, as follow-on to the Trimontium investigation, Drs Simon Clarke and Alicia Wise did a three week excavation at Easter Lilliesleaf, Roxburghshire. Previous years fieldwalking and detecting had produced a reasonable amount of Roman material including coins, jewelry, Samian, black and gray pottery and amphorae and Bradford geophysics had shown one large roundhouse and a smaller one within an enclosure. Although this excavation awaits publication, I can remember that the large roundhouse was overlaid by a rectangular building and that the finds there corresponded with those of the 2nd century annexes at Trimontium.

This did not come as a complete surprise as I had known about the Easter Lilliesleaf site for some years through field-walking finds. It is unusual to find Roman pottery, especially Samian, on a native site, so this was obviously the headman's house and, having worked many years in the area, I knew that there were five palisaded enclosures which showed as cropmarks in the immediate neighbourhood.

This is a likely pattern for native settlements during the Roman periods of occupation. The headman/chief would collect taxes in kind from his followers, pay a portion to the local 'vectigalium exactor' and use the remainder to trade for the pottery etc which we find on the site. Naturally, in dealing with the Trimontium Romans, the headman would copy their method of house building as a status symbol.

The palisaded enclosures are not recorded and field-walking/detecting has produced only three small corroded 3rd/4th century copper coins from them. To me, these are indications that romanisation remained in the Borders longer than the legions did, for I have never believed the numismatic conviction that such coins were booty from south of the border, or bribery or brought back from foreign travel in modern times and subsequently discarded.

THE RURAL COLONIA?

Rectangular buildings were turning up in other places as well. While trying to trace what is known as 'Malcolm's Road', but originally Dere Street, southwards from Lauder to Leaderfoot, I found that the divining rods kept insisting that there were things on either side of the road. These were far too closely together to be fortlets or signal stations, so I investigated. After a lot of checking, I found that they were squarish land plots with sides that varied from 180 to 200m, making a land plot of about five acres or two hectares. This were bounded by a wall and a ditch but the ditch was on the inside, obviously designed to keep animals inside the plot rather than keep them out. Occasionally there was a ditch on both sides of the wall which would keep animals in and out of the plot. This was a field system and seemed fairly uniform in construction although the area enclosed varied with the availability of arable land.

Inside this plot, was a further shape 30m by 20m. Each of these internal shapes faced on to the road with a four metre gateway. Within this 30m x 20m shape were two buildings at one end, a number of postholes along the back wall and a pit, most likely to be a well. The buildings within had broad foundations, likely to be stone and turf walls. Again this was a relatively consistent measurement and I was to find them along the lines of most of my 'Roman' roads.

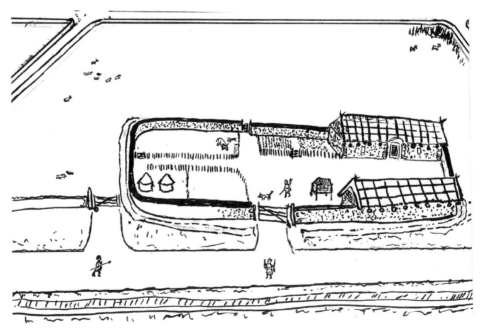

This took my interest for they were obviously land-holdings for a population spread along the lines of communication. I persevered and was finding them all over the place, especially in arable ground. When I got to four hundred of them over an area from Pennymuir to Lauder and Lilliesleaf to Sprouston, I decided that they had to be Roman since nobody else had the organisation, manpower and skill to plan and execute such an ambitious scheme.

This is not simply a wild supposition as there are instances of tribal confederacies numbering hundreds of thousands being moved within the Roman Empire and outside its boundaries into newly conquered territory in order to extend the empire.

I was so intrigued with the internal enclosures of what seemed to be farm steadings that I took three diverse examples and plotted them carefully. Sorrowlessfield Mains is on Dere Street, Torwoodlee Mains on the east/west road to Lyne and Nether Whitlaw on a minor unidentified road. Although not identical, they were sufficiently alike to suggest a standard building pattern.

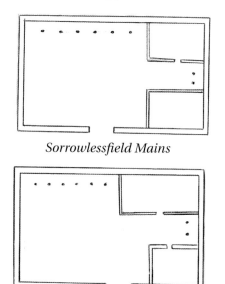

Sorrowlessfield Mains

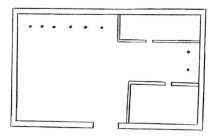

Torwoodlee Mains

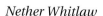

Nether Whitlaw

There are two possible times when this could have happened. One is during the last two decades of the 1st century when it could coincide with the settlement at Easter Happrew which has produced high quality finds, coins and casting waste all 1st century. Although still to be investigated, this is an early vicus, with an imported population planted near the fort for protection. Was there a similar scheme to colonise the surrounding area because there was always a land-hungry population within the Empire and it suited Rome to extend its boundaries?

The second and more probable period was in the early 140s when the new Emperor, Antoninius Pius required a trophy conquest to boost his political prestige. This invasion concentrated on re-occupying southern Scotland and holding it with a new frontier on the Forth-Clyde line, the Antonine Wall. So it made sense for the new area to be settled with a romanised people who would accept the land and duties involved.

Where did they come from? I don't know and, like everybody else, can only guess. A few may have been veterans who had retired from active service and had settled in familiar territory. Most would be natives already here or incomers who were taking the advantage of pax Romana to secure land-owning, and incidentally, taxpaying status. This goes some way to explaining why metal-detectorists are finding Roman coins and brooches in many unsuspected parts of the Borders. These are mainly in the lower-lying arable lands while the upper regions seem to remain in a wild state as pollen analysis confirms. Wild did not necessarily mean unvisited as the skull of an aurochs (huge wild ox) with a Roman spear in it, was dredged up at Whitmuir Loch near Selkirk during draining for marle.

When I mooted a Roman rural colonia, it was received by the archaeological world with a distinct lack of enthusiasm and I got no encouragement to explore the concept further. The idea of a colonia is likely but will be tremendously difficult to prove though it may be acknowledged some day when explainable science catches up with divining rods.

Minor Roads

As well as Dere Street, the main road northwards and the two east/west roads from Craik and Lyne respectively, there are many minor roads throughout the Borders only a few of which have been explored. My criterion for a Roman road is that it has a number of 30m by 20m structures along it within a two hectare (or thereabouts) field system.

In Selkirkshire Book One, p 167, I told of a minor road that linked the east/west road from Craik to the fort at Oakwood. From Gawndie's Knowe **NT 447 174** where there is a likely signal station, traces of a constructed road lead past a faint rectangular enclosure, c 80 metres by 55 metres*, at **NT 440 182**. This could have been a turf-dyke enclosure of the 18th century but when I found the single ditch and wall contained eight rows of pits 8m apart, with the six individual pits separated by 6m spacing in each row, I recognised the pattern of a Roman temporary camp. The tent-pole pattern previously described confirmed the diagnosis. I assumed these temporary camps to a road-making squad although only traces of the road were visible, and these could be of any age.

Following along the tentative line of road, I found a similar camp at **NT 418 207** with a signal tower beside it and another camp with signal station at **NT 416 231**. Further along the road I found that the divined road ran into the Oakwood fort annexe through the gateway at the south-west corner, an unusual arrangement. This ties the date of the road to the second phase of occupation which may have ended c AD 105.

This road is difficult to follow but the late Dr Bill Lonie, who totally distrusted divining rods, got nearly the same line by walking it. My case is strengthened by a row of round cairns at **NT432 187,** along the side of my provisional road.

The same road-making squad was in operation from the Oakwood fort, making towards Dere Street. Similar sized temporary camps were noted at Headshaw New Plantation **464 244**, New Greenhill **490 260**, Whitmuir **498 268**, Houdshall **520 274**. In these four camps the road ran through the middle of them and there may be an undiscovered camp between the first two. At Templehall Plantation, a similar camp was on the roadside at **530 280**.

I stopped mapping there but an extension of the road on the same line passed the Samian sherd and the hoard of Kippielaw coins mentioned above.

*This paced measurement was wrong. On checking this line of road in 2011, I discovered that there were two camps occupying the same ground but on different alignments. In fact both fitted into the Roman 'iugerum' which are mentioned above.

With this mistake, the rest needed checking and I found that they all had been re-jigged at some time but all fitted into the iugerum measurements. At the Headshaw site there were two camps end to end along a ridge. Of course the 'road-making' squad may have been pioneers making the field systems and farm steadings above mentioned.

Having solved the problem of the iugerum at Innerleithen to my own satisfaction, I was pleased to find that the pattern fitted equally well along the minor road from Gawndie's Knowe to Oakwood fort and eastwards from there.

But it came as a bit of a surprise when I was checking round the several temporary camps at Milrighall, near Midlem and found six iugera which conformed to size but not to purpose. These were on a slight slope and had the standard twelve tent-sites in the upper half. In the bottom half, there were two rows of posts about 2m apart running down the middle of the bottom half. My best guess would be that these would be cavalry quarters with the troopers on the higher ground and the horses in the lower half, either under some form of roofing or simply tied in cavalry lines. Or they might simply be standard sized fields which had not been previously noted.

ROUND HOUSES

The advent of rectangular houses did not drive out the conservative taste for round houses. As noted above, round houses are difficult to date as they range from Bronze Age to medieval times but if you find them clustered near a Roman fort or beside a Roman road, they are likely to be 1st/2nd century.

Of course, the best method of dating the round house is to find a hoard of Roman coins in or near it. I have been lucky enough to be involved in the Roman hoards of Edston, Kippielaw and Synton , each of which was near roundhouse settlements.

Although round houses are easily picked up by divining rods, they seldom show on air photographs. With the wooden structure of the house vanished through time, only the floor remains. This is only visible on air photographs in dry conditions and if the field has seldom been ploughed. On the few round house excavations I have seen, I noted that the initial basis of the floor was of puddle clay which is damp-proof and then packed with stones to make a hard floor which is impenetrable for deep-rooting plants.

I did say at the beginning that rabbits and moles were archaeological aids; so are plants but they are most useful in fields which have not been ploughed for generations. A parched circle in a field of permanent grass can indicate a roundhouse although care has to be taken not to confuse these with the marks left by circular cattle-feeding troughs.

Many of the metal-detectorist finds of Roman coins and brooches from non-Roman sites are from native roundhouse settlements but extensive cultivation has made it difficult to determine where major settlements were located. Most of our knowledge of roundhouses comes from excavation on hilly sites.

CHAPTER ELEVEN

~~The End~~

This is not the end of the story but, in fact, is only an interim report of work in progress. So why publish a book which is not even half-written yet? The answer is that I will be seventy-eight by the time this hits the booksellers' counters and with no certainty of reaching seventy-nine, I thought it best to put what I have seen/discovered/thought down on paper to be dissected by those who know much, but wish to know more about the archaeology and history of the Borders.

I bear in mind the fact that a number of eminent archaeologists have still to publish the reports of excavations they did thirty or forty years ago. While sympathising with their desire to get everything absolutely correct, I feel that they are doing their profession a disservice by keeping that knowledge to themselves. However, archaeology is a punishing profession and a single slight mistake can diminish a lifetime's reputation.

On the other hand, there are those like Professor St Joseph whose enthusiasm in the fields of air photography of archaeological sites were so great that he often could not spare the time to write up his findings. When he died at the age of eighty-two, it was written that: *"He published much but left much more unpublished"*. Fortunately, his remaining unpublished works were carefully annotated and his notebooks are now in capable hands. Thus his work is not lost to future generations.

With neither a reputation to consider, nor a profession to protect, this is literally a 'publish and be damned' attempt to add a fresh insight to what is there and still to be found. I know it is raw in content and illustration but it is published to inform rather than impress. I think I am right in everything herein but am quite willing to be proved wrong. In which case, I wait to be convinced and can always fall back on my usual defence that I am but 'a poor but honest wood-cutter' and nothing much can be expected of me.

ADDENDUM

Having finished with the Roman forts, camps etc. in the Borders, I was taken to see the souterrain at Crichton Mains which, as its name says, is under the ground. A long passage with many dressed Roman stones in it, this type of structure has been identified variously from an underground storage to a temple. It has been deduced that there must have been a Roman fort in the immediate vicinity to provide that number of stones.

I was most impressed, for even though the souterrain had been re-built in the 19th century, there was a strange atmosphere about it. While casting about to see if it came from a building, as the Trimontium ones did, I found that it had originally stood within a 27m square enclosure. Although the walls of this had been stone-robbed, probably to build the souterrain, they had been nearly 1m thick. These should have shown up on air photographs as a slight depression round the building but plough-drop at the end of each furrow would disguise this.

From its location and shape, I would say that this is most likely to have been a temple site.

There was a potential Roman fort site about half a mile away and I was tempted towards it even though the field was in sprouting corn. As this temptation was hard to resist, I found a 90m by 60m fort at **NT40078 62414** with an annexe to the west. I did find the accompanying bathhouse and latrine but never got them GPS-ed as I was asked politely, but justifiably, to leave the field. *Peccavi. Mea culpa.* Sorry.

Well, that seems to be as far as I can go with the Romans, so it is on to the Dark Ages, now known as Early Historic. And geology looks interesting too.